Profitable
Negotiation

Profitable Negotiation

Gavin Kennedy

ORION
BUSINESS
BOOKS

For Felix

Copyright © 1999 by Gavin Kennedy

The right of Gavin Kennedy to be identified as the
author of this work has been asserted by him in accordance with the
Copyright, Designs and Patents Act 1988.

This edition first published in Great Britain in 1999 by
Orion Business
An imprint of The Orion Publishing Group Ltd
Orion House, 5 Upper St Martin's Lane, London WC2H 9EA

A CIP catalogue record for this book
is available from the British Library

ISBN 0–75281–357–9

Typeset by Deltatype Ltd, Birkenhead, Merseyside
Printed and bound in Great Britain by
Clays Ltd, St. Ives plc

Contents

5 Decisions, decisions

6 Risking trust

7 Jousting with Slobovic

8 Sitting next to Nellie

9 What do we want?

15 Competitive and co-operative bargaining strategies

16 Alongside negotiation

Appendix The Negotek® Competence Test

Chapter 1
Introduction

➡ WHO SHOULD READ THIS BOOK?

Fortunately for social cohesion and our personal freedoms, we engage in behaviours we call negotiation.

What would it be like if we went back to 'top down' management and 'bottom up' deference and fear? Certainly, those who lived through the last decades of that kind of world (and those who still live in its shadow) do not hanker to return to them. Whatever else such a traumatic reversal would achieve, it would not merely replace today's problems with yesterday's but add to them. People, having lost their unquestioned – and unquestionable – deference, are unlikely to revert voluntarily.

So, we live in an age when negotiation in all contexts is widely practised. Unfortunately, however, for our prosperity and our self-worth, we are not always good at negotiating. We negotiate to get things done and, because we hardly think about how we negotiate, we do it less well than we might. And it shows where it matters in our people management and in the pursuit of our interests.

This book is not for the accomplished negotiating practitioner. For these readers, I have written other books, such as *The New Negotiating Edge* (Nicholas Brealey, 1998) and *Kennedy on Negotiation* (Gower, 1998). The behavioural tools set out here are for negotiators who have a serious intention to improve. You may feel consciously 'incompetent' as a negotiator and, though probably you exaggerate your deficiencies, you intend to become at least consciously competent. In short, you want some tools to negotiate better.

You won't find this book a route to instant success, nor am I about to show you the so-called 'secrets' of doing Big Deals. I am not writing for high-powered wheeler-dealers, nor for dreamers. Instead, you get a survey of negotiating behaviour, plus proven tools, that will help you the next time you look into the eyes of someone who thinks they have got your measure.

At Edinburgh Business School we practise the edict that knowledge transfer takes the form of 'concept–example–practise'. A concept unsupported by an example is of little value to a practitioner. And examples you cannot practise are not worth much either. Thus, for every concept, I provide an example and for every example I invite you to practise the application of the concept (excepting, of course, in repetitive cases).

So, you must decide if this is the appropriate level of book for you. If you have already paid for it, please do not feel obliged to continue reading. Economists (of which I am one) preach that 'bygones are bygones', because money once spent is gone for ever. Reading a book that is not for you – 'because otherwise it is a waste' – is not wise; if you compound the waste of your money with a waste of your time, you are in need of a toolkit in basic economics, and perhaps one in time management too. Hence, if this is the wrong text for you, the rational choice is to stop reading it and to do something more useful (such as read one of my other books?).

Throughout the chapters there are numerous 'Activities', which invite you to contemplate aspects of your experience that might relate to the topic under discussion. Try to carry out the set task, even briefly, and avoid jumping over the Activities to the text. Relevant comments follow the Activities and these assume that you have at least tried to carry out the set tasks. Each Activity is intended to enrich your learning by involving you and your experience or opinions with the concepts and behavioural tools of negotiation, and they are as close to practising the examples as you can get from reading a book.

At the end of each chapter, the behavioural tools it has introduced are summarised in a section called 'For your toolkit'. Mostly, these are practical tools for you to use but sometimes they are also attitudinal. I have tried to avoid non-functional tools like 'be aware', 'be alert' and so on. I have also included some negative advice in the form of 'don'ts'. There is a school of training that criticises the use of 'don'ts' on the grounds that you should always teach what the student is to do positively and not divert their attention into teaching what not to do.

I remain sceptical about such fads, especially among professional trainers, where the necessary repetition of the same material invokes a constant search for new angles to jazz up presentations. For the trainee, the trainer's message is pristine, new and not repetitive, and they do not share their trainer's boredom threshold. The effect of the message on the recipient is the decisive test for me. For example, which is most effective as a guide to behaviour, the negative injunction, 'Don't drink and drive', or the faddish compliant, 'Only drive while sober'? Given that the temptation to drink precedes the opportunity to drive, the force of the injunction is better placed in the negative form of 'Don't drink'. Hence, 'Don't interrupt' is a superior behavioural injunction to saying something like: 'Ony speak when nobody else is speaking'.

Lastly, I have included Negotiate's Negotek® Multiple Choice Competence Test at the end of the book for you to complete. It is best if you attempt the test after you have read the book and under the constraint not to look for the answers before choosing from the options! A fair pass would give you 8 correct answers out of 12 and 10 out of 12 is much better (I would be suspicious of 12 out of 12, but then idealist examiners are virgin cynics!). If you would like me to comment on your answers, or if you have any comments on the book and its concepts and tools, please contact me at the address given at the back of the book.

➡ WHAT IS NEGOTIATION BEHAVIOUR?

Activity 1.1

For those for whom this book clearly serves their interests and who intend to continue reading it, think about and then answer the question· What does the word 'negotiate' mean for you?

I prefer functional to philosophical definitions as tools. When I want a light on in a dark room, I prefer to press switches without testing for Ohm's law. My definition (not found in a dictionary) of negotiation as behaviour is functional:

The process by which we search for terms to obtain what we want from someone who wants something from us.

Your tools in your toolkit reveal that process and identify the associated *behaviours* that usually work effectively – and a few that don't – in pursuit of the negotiated *results* you seek. They identify how your attitudes to *relationships* influence your behaviour when you seek to obtain what you want from someone who wants something from you. You will also see what happens when the other person does not want anything at all from you, and what you can or cannot do about it.

Sometimes you read definitions too quickly and if mine is read too quickly, errors result. For example, erroneous ideas and practices come from only applying the first part ('obtain what you want from someone') in isolation from the second part ('who wants something from you').

When you are solely concerned with the first part of the definition, your behaviour changes negotiation from an *exchange* of what each of you wants from the other into one where you expect them to give you what you want for nothing – in other words everything for you and nothing for them. You behave as a '*taker*'.

Activity 1.2

When was the last time you behaved as a 'taker' by not considering the wants of the other party? Perhaps you felt you were in the driving seat and behaved as if they needed you more than you needed them?

Can you remember the last time that you were on the receiving end of a taker's negotiating behaviour (all for them, nothing much for you)? How did you feel about them exploiting you?

Conversely, supplying only what someone wants from you in isolation from what you want from them also leads to poor practice. When you are solely concerned with the second part of the definition, your behaviour also changes negotiation from an exchange into one where you give them what they want and you expect nothing from them in return – i.e. everything for them and nothing for you. You behave as a 'giver'.

Have you been a 'giver' recently, downplaying your wants to give somebody else what they want – perhaps to keep the peace, to avoid trouble, or because you felt too weak and didn't know what to do about it?

Do you find yourself giving most of the time, or do you give to suit the circumstances?

To protect yourself from becoming a taker or a giver (each set of behaviours has its strengths and weaknesses), you must 'search for terms'.

Negotiation is a search, not a promise – you seek a settlement but might not find it. Not all negotiations succeed with both of you obtaining what you want. You may fail to find agreeable terms and, make no mistake, unless the terms are agreeable you should 'fail to agree'.

'Succeeding' usually means concluding the negotiation with an exchange, though this does not require you to agree just because if you didn't it would be a failure. Some 'failed' negotiations succeed, because the parties avoid a poor, or even a bad, deal and the inevitable regrets. For example, you accept an offer for your house, well below your aspirations, because you panic when nobody else views the property. Two days after you conclude the sale, potential buyers call, saying yours is just the house they want and they promptly offer more than your original asking price.

➡ WHAT HAPPENS IN NEGOTIATION?

Why do negotiators behave the way they do?

Suppose you observe two people, one the manager of a professional football club and the other a player's agent, negotiating a signing on fee for the new season. Unlike football itself, with its strict laws and a refereeing system to enforce them, no rules and no referees govern the conduct of negotiations. Yet both sides appear to abide by unwritten and powerful conventions – they do not hit each other, for example, though there might be much shouting and abusive language.

The conventions, including the rituals and theatricals – buyers opening 'low' and sellers opening 'high' – are observable. Each plays a 'game', so to speak, and seems to know it *is* a game: they exaggerate, make allegations, bob and weave, thrust and parry, threaten to leave, and generally mix it with the mental agility of two gladiators. Each plays a role, though neither admits to it.

Some behaviours are acquired from the vagaries of fashion. Agents drive large black limousines and flaunt their social life with big-name players and rock stars; managers boast of the 'tight ship' they run and flaunt their power over their signed players. Both like talking big numbers as if it is small change.

The football authorities, the legal system and the tax authorities impose regulations and norms supposedly governing the conduct of the manager and the player's agent. These external constraints are real, and both parties sometimes behave as if the authorities were present at the table, with each reminding the other that they can't agree to this or that because 'it's against the Rules'. At other times they take advantage of an absence of the authorities, with the agent suggesting ways of evading the tax rules and the manager suggesting ways to mislead the football authorities.

Both parties change the constraints on the negotiating game if it is to their advantage, and both adapt to changes imposed externally and beyond their control. If the manager gets it right more often than he gets it wrong, his team prospers; if the agent gets it right more times than she gets it wrong, her clients prosper. In both cases, if the team prospers, the players prosper, and the manager and the agent prosper too.

Unfortunately, there is no guarantee of such happy symmetries in negotiated outcomes.

Activity 1.4

What is the worst deal (business or personal) that you ever concluded and one that you still regret?

Can you recall why you accepted the offer? Were you desperate?

Misled? Naïve? Or was it that you accepted the offer because it seemed to be more important to you at the time than it was later?

In every negotiation you conduct, there is a possibility of your succeeding – your search for terms produces an agreeable deal or you avoid one that isn't. And that suggests another implication that is well worth remembering when you are under pressure, which is described in the next section.

➡ THE VETO

Negotiation is a *voluntary* process; it is not compulsory. You can say 'no' (though some ways of saying 'no' are better than others!) and because either party can veto the terms and each retains this residual power, you can't force them to agree to your terms and they can't force you to agree to theirs.

You cannot write your own pay cheque (would that you could!), nor can you fill your supermarket trolley with goodies and pay the checkout whatever sum comes into your head. I hear, though, that there is a restaurant in Edinburgh that allows its customers on Tuesday nights to eat what they want and pay what they think it is worth – but apparently almost everybody pays the menu prices, and some pay even more!

True, there are consequences from rejecting the terms. For a start, you must live without whatever it was that you wanted from them. Hopefully, you may get what you want from somebody else and your failed search with one person succeeds with someone else. But if you absolutely must have whatever it is you want from them, this might cause you to consider the consequences of hastily rejecting their terms. Perhaps you would be better off continuing to negotiate? Thus, for example, a management determined not to pay a penny over $40 an hour for IT specialists, might relax its determination if it fails to recruit or retain anybody: it may only have a realistic choice, say, between offering more than $40 an hour or of only finding substitute IT labour by transferring its IT operations off shore.

Activity 1.5

Recollect a negotiation in which you dramatically changed your intentions or offer during it because what you started with just would not work.

Can you recall the thinking that led you to realise that your plans were awry? Whom did you have to convince that a substantial change was necessary? Why did you get it so 'wrong'? Was it that they convinced you to move? When did you realise you had moved too far?

For your toolkit

T1.1 Always apply the functional definition of negotiation behaviour: 'The process by which we search for terms to obtain what we want from someone who wants something from us.'

T1.2 You can succeed in your negotiations *either* by agreeing to the offered terms *or* by rejecting them.

T1.3 You may veto the offered terms.

T1.4 You may propose different terms.

T1.5 You may volunteer to accept their terms.

T1.6 You may reject unsatisfactory deals – if you cannot bring yourself to do this from the start, you will always settle on less satisfactory terms than those available.

Chapter 2
Why do we negotiate?

➡ A REDUNDANT QUESTION

In one sense this is a redundant question. Humans negotiate and that's that. The answer will not change the necessity for humans to negotiate from time to time. Redundant questions, however, are worthy of an answer when they provide insights into behaviour.

As in the fairy tale of the Emperor's new clothes, in which nobody except the little boy questioned what they were doing, science has long struggled against accepting the obvious. 'Obviously' the Sun goes round the Earth; the Earth is flat; heavy objects fall faster than lighter ones; the Earth is at the centre of the Universe, and so on! (Don't laugh; our predecessors believed passionately in these 'obvious' truths and pilloried – or worse – those who didn't.)

➡ CULTURAL RELATIVISM OR UNIVERSAL BEHAVIOUR?

In behavioural science, too, remarkably productive counter-intuitive questions abound. Many business authors, for example, believe that each culture negotiates differently (practitioners, I find, are less clear-cut). This 'must be true', the authors allege, because there are obvious and significant differences between a village Chinese and an urban European. Surely these differences are cultural imperatives and *must* affect how Chinese and Europeans negotiate?

To question why some undeniably significant differences, such as language, change negotiation behaviour risks ridicule from those who believe in the obvious. Many books on culture and negotiation confuse what is significant with what is important, and it is worth risking ridicule to ask why they make this elementary mistake.

Activity 2.1

A Californian makes a sales presentation to a group of Asians and when she has finished there is silence. She covers her embarrassment by slicing her price. There is still silence. So she makes another concession, and another, as the silence continues. After ten minutes of silence, which has produced significant concessions from her, she gives up and slumps back in her seat. The Asians leave the room.

Is this an example of a cultural misunderstanding – Asians culturally do not react immediately, etc., whereas Americans culturally expect an instant response and she was ignorant of the cultural differences? If you believe it is and she was, then you are a cultural relativist. I also think you confuse what is undeniably a negotiating error in any culture with a trait allegedly applicable in only one culture.

Is this an example of a negotiating – rather than a cultural – error on her part when she makes unilateral concessions without first receiving a response from the Asians? If you believe it is, then you are a universalist. I also think you are likely to become a competent negotiator who will do well when negotiating with Asians or Californians.

To help you when dealing with negotiators who use a silence ploy, you can practise dealing with silence by counting to five after somebody speaks and when it is your turn to respond. Practise this twenty times in the next 24 hours.

➡ **SOCIAL EVOLUTION**

So I press the question: why do humans negotiate, and why only humans among all the animals?

Animals distribute the bounties of nature, which includes each other, by violence or the threat of violence or, more accurately, by 'dominance and display'. If an animal can deter the rest of a group from challenging (usually, but not always) him, then he takes his pick of food, mates and territory.

Natural selection capitalises on minute changes to the status quo, some of which survive but most of which lead to dead ends. Changes in the status quo successfully replicate when the organisms carrying the changes live long enough to breed more successfully than those without it. That is why, over time, changes spread throughout a population, and why also some changes disappear. Whether the changes are in any sense 'improvements' is not relevant.

Activity 2.2

How many fads and fashions have you been subjected to as a manager in the past five years? Can you remember such fashions as 'management by objectives', 'productivity pay', 'quality circles', 'performance-related pay', 'total quality management', 'downsizing', 'rightsizing', 'reengineering', 'empowerment' and '360° assessments'?

What are they calling the fads you must cope with this month? Why do you think there are so many temporary fads and why do they come and go so quickly?

Despite the 'obvious' belief that evolution progresses ever upwards to some better state of life, the 'obvious' belief is by no means correct: evolution is not purposely going anywhere, be it upwards, sideways or downwards. Humans for now, and perhaps accidentally, are the highest form of intelligent life, but measured in evolutionary time the human species may not survive 80,000 years, while the humble dolphin may well reach its sixth millionth birthday quite easily.

The science of biological evolution is only controversial among flat-earthers and those who remain prisoners of those with vested interests in perpetuating myths and superstition. This was brought home to me recently on a visit to the beautiful Santa Croce, in Florence, when I stood by the tomb of Galileo and pondered how stupid were the persecutors of his 'crimes' against their supposedly heavenly authority.

Social evolution unsurprisingly is less controversial among scientists and lay people alike. There can be little doubt that societies have changed within the last 50 years, let alone the last 40,000. I suggest that they evolve under pressures similar to natural selection. Moreover, I suggest that every conceivable variation on any social or societal norm is, or has been, or will be, experimented with by members of the human species and, despite Francis Fukuyama's brilliant essay, *The End of History*, future generations and epochs will continue to experiment. In this, I incline to the side of the Jewish preacher Ecclesiastes, who elaborated on the theme that 'there is no new thing under the sun'.

The human species has achieved remarkable changes in social relationships over its relatively short history. Our *social* evolution has been spectacular, and one significant and important manifestation of our successful social evolution is the very human capacity to negotiate.

Negotiating behaviour is a product of natural selection and its dissemination in its modern forms is a product of social evolution. A proclivity for food sharing in families and small bands raised the chances of surviving the vagaries of the food supply. It was not possible for small groups of humans (or their hominid predecessors) to survive by engaging in a 'war of all against all'; the acquisition of the necessary intelligence to practise primitive co-operation laid the foundations for larger human societies to evolve the capacity to negotiate.

You can see this in two related phenomena. For one, negotiation has never had a monopoly of human decision making. For thousands of years, negotiation was a minority activity indulged in when events dictated that it was prudent to negotiate rather than to pillage. What is new is that negotiation is now a near-majority activity coexisting with competing forms of decision making. For a second, shadow remnants of violent intimidatory conduct permeate negotiating practice, seen in the continuing reliance of some people on browbeating and intimidation.

Activity 2.3

Think of someone who tends to intimidate to get what he or she wants from you. How do you feel when subjected to their treatment?

Have you ever intimidated anybody to get what you want? Think of the circumstances that led to your intimidation of others.

When precisely our ancestors explicitly exchanged something for something else, rather than use a heavy stone to crush a stranger's skull, is, and will ever remain, a tantalising mystery. The first acts of explicit trade probably exchanged female sexual favours for meat provided by male hunters (the first occurrence of the division of labour), perhaps foreshadowed as an exchange process familiar to our primate cousins in the behaviour we call 'grooming'. Humans are not so much 'naked ape' as 'negotiating ape'!

Explicit trade did not end violent behaviour, but trade grew in volume and that is all that social evolution needed to do its work. Unlike biological evolution, which is totally confined to the individual, who has no sense of what is 'good for the species', social evolution works through the group rather than the individual. A collective memory, some parts of which we call knowledge, spreads through the open access of language to all individuals and, thereby, spreads much faster than biological evolution, which takes thousands of generations to change a species. Since the agricultural revolution, no political system has lasted thousands of generations.

➡ BENEFITS OF TRADE

Slowly, imperceptibly almost, barter and exchange replicated throughout our species. Eventually, all human groups practised trade activities in one form or another. By the fifteenth century, so firmly established was trade that many disasters (mainly wars and genocide, but also social experiments such as communism) failed to reverse the spread of trading behaviours. The elements of negotiation became more sophisticated compared with the primitive exchanges initiated by our unknown ancestors, but were not essentially different.

Absolute rulers, even when self-sanctified to be of divine

attribution, are subject to challenges. If an absolute ruler is forced to consult with those of lesser rank (*Magna Carta*, for instance) rather than kill them, what was once absolute becomes relative. And we see in recent history how limited rights to negotiate minor issues have inexorably spread to more extensive agendas: truly, everything is becoming negotiable. (Academic colleagues tell me that some students now try to negotiate their final examination grades!)

Activity 2.4

Ask someone at least thirty years older than you to reminisce about their early work experiences.

Ask them how they were told what to do by their bosses, what would have been the result of refusing to comply or 'cheeking' back, and search for examples of what they considered to be injustices in their treatment at school, university, work or from government agencies.

Get a feel for the world they were brought up in and then compare their memories of their world with images of yours. Allow for doses of nostalgia, even firm defences of codes and rules common in 'their day', and ignore mocking despair at how 'easy today's young have it'!

In today's society, negotiation is the norm and not the exception. Our society could not function so well without its predilection for negotiation. Competing élites do not volunteer to allow rivals to permanently adopt and impose policies that worsen or threaten their lifestyles. That is one of the reasons that finally undermined apartheid among the whites of South Africa, and turned affluent '60s drop-outs in the West off 'flower power' and its associated nonsense. Eventually – even if it takes many years or decades – people, through social evolution, try something more favourable to their interests.

So why do we negotiate? The short answer is because it works and what works replicates. The alternatives – including violence, autocracy, top-down management, government dictat, commissars, priests, mullahs and coercion – are ever-present but no longer dominant, except locally. Ultimately they are, and will remain, unsuccessful.

And the one great truth about how we live in this age of negotiation has not escaped, and cannot be hidden from, the attention of billions of humans: those societies that create and distribute the bounties of nature and the fruits of labour by voluntary negotiation in all cases (there are no exceptions) grow wealthier than those societies that apply other principles. We negotiate, therefore, not just because it is an option, but because it is in our interests so to do.

For your toolkit

T2.1 Avoid accepting culturally specific explanations for poor negotiating behaviour – it is sufficient for you to correct the negotiating errors.

T2.2 Effective negotiating behaviours are universal – and so are the errors.

T2.3 Do not move from your opening position without first receiving a response from the other side.

T2.4 If it is their turn to respond, keep quiet and endure the silence no matter how long it lasts (and thirty seconds is a long time). They feel as much pressure as you to end the silence, unless, like the only fish ever to be caught by anglers, you cannot keep your mouth shut.

T2.5 Use a 10-, or even 20-second silence whenever you ask questions, respond to a question, suggest proposals, offer bargains, or when it is your turn to speak.

T2.6 Negotiating, for all its costs, works better than its rivals, but you must endure the costs to reap the benefits.

Chapter 3
Your attitudes

➡ YOUR EXPERIENCE

I confidently assert that you already have considerable experience
of negotiation. My confidence may surprise you because you may
not yet see yourself as a negotiator – after all, that is why you are
reading this book about negotiation! But as an adult you have
spent many years negotiating with those close to you: your family,
your friends and your social partners.

You do not, therefore, come to negotiation totally inexper-
ienced. You may not consider yourself to be totally competent, but
you have negotiated to a greater extent than you imagine. That is
why I am also confident that you have formed attitudes about how
to negotiate. Your attitudes drive your negotiating behaviour and
guide you as surely as if you consciously followed them.

➡ MODELLING ATTITUDES

A model is a concept. The one I use is simplicity itself. Briefly, it
links behaviour and attitudes in a single diagram. Figure 3.1 shows
two boxes labelled 'Behaviour' and 'Attitudes'. The boxes overlap
because they imperfectly match.

Your attitudes imperfectly drive your behaviour. You could, if
you are a certain male type for example, allege that 'women are
dangerous drivers' and jump a red light next Saturday morning.
You might justify your dangerous behaviour with the excuse that
you are in a hurry, but that won't alter your ridiculous prejudices.

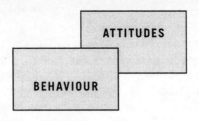

Figure 3.1 Behaviour and attitudes

Attitudes are always close to the surface. You are normally unreserved when circumstances provoke you to express them. In common discourse, too, you reveal your attitudes and you argue against the interpretations put upon them by others.

Conversations without the expression of attitudes are short, informal and, boringly safe. Conversations spiked with attitudes are risky. They are the main filter through which you separate those whom you want to be with from those whom you would never tire of kicking.

Some of your attitudes conflict with your behaviour, but this need not be a public problem because you are able to be deceptive about your attitudes. You can speak for effect – to shock or to please. As nobody can see inside your head, you can mislead, be two-faced, lie and dissemble to suit your convenience (or safety). Sometimes, also, deception is a small price for 'peace'.

Activity 3.1

Think of an attitude that you profess in public to hold but that you have either severe private reservations about, or profoundly disagree with, or you know to be contrary to your real feelings. It could be a business stance, a personal relationship, some social convention, a public expression, a sexual preference, or some doubts about publicly approved ethics or morality.

Rehearse to yourself how you justify the discrepancy between your public and your private attitudes.

How attitudinally duplicitous you are in practice only you know, and people – unfairly or otherwise – may credit you with a greater capacity for deceit than you may recognise. (Perhaps they deceive you about their true attitudes too?)

This does not make you necessarily a moral defective, nor should you take umbrage at my assertions. Some people profess to believe that a person should never pretend to hold one attitude when they actually believe the opposite, but they usually live in open societies where the penalty for expressing one's true beliefs are not as severe as they are in totalitarian societies (or totalitarian families – think of the painful dilemmas of revealing one's sexuality compared with hiding it).

Human interactions vary, and some degree of what I allege about attitudes and behaviour almost certainly applies to you. Your current attitudes towards those with whom you negotiate drive your behaviour. As this can have profound effects when you negotiate, it is as well that you understand the dynamics of interacting with others. In adding to your toolkit, you do not have time for timidity or self-delusion.

Activity 3.2

Consider the following statement and assess how closely it fits with your attitudes: 'In business a man with money meets a man with experience; the man with the experience ends up with the money and the man with the money ends up with the experience.'

How true is this of what happens in business? Has it happened to you? If yes, would you be happy to let it happen again? Has it happened to somebody you know, but not to you? And if yes, would you allow it to happen to you?

What would you do to prevent it happening (again)?

Note, the statement is a cynical line from a B-movie. To the extent that it could be true, you should be on your guard against cheats. But with that attitude, how might you behave when you think you are dealing with a 'man with experience'?

Do you see how pervasive *your* attitudes can be?

Broadly stated, you have a set of attitudes towards people and what they are about and these attitudes guide your behaviour when you interact with them. As you gain more experience of specific types of interaction, such as negotiation, you refine your behaviour and become set in your ways. If your behaviours work well, you repeat them; if they don't, you avoid situations where you must use them.

Avoidance behaviours are commonly resorted to in many social contexts. Some people, for instance, cannot stand parties or socialising with colleagues, clients or relatives, or they have no small talk and yearn to be rescued from contact with the *hoi polloi*.

Thus, while some people always haggle over a seller's price, others avoid like the plague challenging somebody else's choice of what is good for them. In the appropriate context of a tourist market, say, those who normally incline towards avoidance of haggling behaviour, haggle because it is the 'done thing' and it is fun. In the hotel dining room that night, tourists at every table regale each other with their daring deals for trinkets. When they return home, the trinket they haggled over sits forlornly on a shelf and they return to their avoidance habit of never challenging a fixed price: they readopt the set of attitudes that causes them to avoid haggling behaviours.

➡ YOUR ATTITUDES AFFECT YOUR NEGOTIATING

There is no escape from the links between attitudes and behaviour, though you can change your attitudes (through the influence of persuasion and experience) and you can change your behaviour (through training and practice).

I contend that uninformed negotiating behaviour falls into one of two common kinds (there is a third, less common but more effective, kind, of which much more later).

Activity 3.3

Read the following statements and decide whether you think they are True (T) or False (F).

---

1. *Negotiators do best if they concentrate on winning.*   T   F

2. *When someone is clearly factually incorrect, it saves time if you can correct their errors straight away.*   T   F

3. *It is usually only worth negotiating if your opponent is being reasonable.*   T   F

4. *I might as well walk out if my opponent won't accept my reasonable proposals.*   T   F

5. *Just because they say something is non-negotiable is no reason to drop it.*   T   F

These are only a small sample of a negotiator's possible attitudes, but they reveal quite a lot about your attitudinal stances and your likely associated behaviours. Of course, linkages only indicate how you might behave, and it is not imperative for you to behave in one particular way in all circumstances.

First, some brief comments on the attitudes behind your choices.

1. *Negotiators do best if they concentrate on winning.*
   If you marked this as True, you see negotiation as analogous to competitive sport, where the winner does measurably better than the loser(s). The buyer does well who buys cheapest and the seller does well who sells dearest. If you marked it False, perhaps the word 'winning' worried you because you don't see winning as the most important result of a negotiation; you don't feel comfortable winning at somebody else's expense.

2. *When someone is clearly factually incorrect, it saves time if you can correct their errors straight away.*
   If you recognise some statements that are clearly factually incorrect, and you want to avoid wasting time, you could rush to correct them straight away, perhaps even interrupting to do so. How many arguments begin in disputes over so-called 'facts'? What are the *positive* consequences associated with interrupting? I have

never met anyone who likes to be interrupted – but nor have I met anyone who has not interrupted somebody else!

3. *It is usually only worth negotiating if your opponent is being reasonable.*

   The word 'opponent' carries attitudinal baggage. It reflects your perception of the people with whom you do business. They are 'opponents', not suppliers, customers, employees, colleagues, neighbours, etc., and you treat them as if you are aiming for the 'winner's' prize.

4. *I might as well walk out if my opponent won't accept my reasonable proposals.*

   There is that word 'opponent' again. And it's remarkable how it is always you who make 'reasonable' proposals rather than the other party to the negotiations. Maybe they won't accept your proposals because they do not share your views on what is reasonable? As for walking out, what does that achieve? Do you expect them to run after you and accept your 'reasonable' offer? And if they don't, is it their fault they must do without whatever you are offering?

5. *Just because they say something is non-negotiable is no reason to drop it.*

   This is a tricky one. A mere claim that something is 'non-negotiable' certainly is no reason on its own for you to drop it – otherwise you teach people to claim this or that is non-negotiable to provoke your submissive response. In my view, trying to force somebody to negotiate on an issue, which for them is beyond consideration, is fraught with risk and suggests arrogance. Neither party can unilaterally set the agenda and enforce it without it ceasing to be a process of negotiation.

➡ RED AND BLUE

For operational simplicity, I classify attitudes to negotiation by the colours red and blue. These are neutral labels compared with other pairings such as 'competitive' or 'co-operative'; 'selfish' or 'altruistic'; 'masculine' or 'feminine'; or 'claiming' or 'creating' – each of which pair brings confusing baggage. Moreover, when translating complex words, unintended meanings appear in other languages,

whereas the labels 'red' and 'blue' take the same meanings in all
languages because these colours are universal.

To demonstrate (as a first cut) how the labels apply to the
statements in Activity 3.3, assign red to all the statements you
marked as True and blue to all the statements you marked as
False.

Crudely, red attitudes distil from a domineering approach to
other people. The extreme limit of the 'red' way to solve a problem
is to intimidate, threaten, force, coerce and generally dominate the
other person. Negotiating is regarded as 'war by other means', and
this view of negotiation is closest to violence and cohabits in the
attitudes of those given to it.

As crudely put, extreme 'blue' attitudes distil from a submissive
approach (because red negotiators successfully intimidate blue
negotiators). Blues submit under pressure for 'peace' – sometimes
at any price – and they abhor the tensions and stresses of conflict.

Be clear though, between the extreme stances there is a long
continuum composed of shades of red and blue, so think of the
colours as organising tools rather than precise definitions carefully
crafted by the scientific rules of a taxonomy. Across the negotiating table, the verbal interaction is too fast-moving for high-order
interpretative subtleties. You need tools to recognise what is
happening quickly and as quickly to help form your response.

The red player sees negotiation as a process in which the parties
divide a fixed pie, with the proviso and intention that the red
player takes the biggest slice. 'More for me means less for you', is
the red player's attitude, with all the implications for their
behaviour that follows from that goal. A red player negotiates
with 'opponents', who are rivals for whatever is in contention. If
pressure by a red player is not working on an opponent, that
merely means that enough pressure is not being applied – so a red
player increases the pressure! Better still, a red player steps it up
anyway, just in case the other party has not got the message that
they must accommodate red demands – or else.

In Activity 3.2, the red player is the one with the manipulative experience who ends up with the money. It is 'tough out there' and red players do not lose gracefully. Meanwhile, if their opponents can't stand the heat, perhaps they should get into another line of work?

Blue players take a different stance. They see good in everyone and negotiate with 'partners', 'friends' and 'honourable' persons, not opponents. ('A stranger is a friend you have not yet met' is typical of blue attitudes.) Blue players avoid tension by conceding trivial things – and then by conceding bigger things. They smooth ruffled feathers by humouring any 'difficult' party (much as a pet dog fawns for its owner's attention).

Now, I have presented red and blue in such unflattering language deliberately. There is a danger that in recoiling from red attitudes you incorrectly attribute to moderate blue attitudes warmer qualities than I intended. It is not the case that red is bad and blue is good; neither red nor blue is morally or ethically superior to the other. They are descriptions of sets of attitudes and not prescriptions for which attitudes you should hold, for I am in the business of disseminating knowledge not piety. But for the practitioner, a knowledge of red and blue attitudes is working data to use while negotiating.

Activity 3.5

Taking my descriptions of red and blue attitudes, where would you place yourself on a continuum between extreme red through to extreme blue on Figure 3.2? What is the colour, or shade of colour, of your natural behaviour? Mark yourself on the continuum below:

| EXTREME RED | MODERATE RED | MODERATE BLUE | EXTREME BLUE |

Figure 3.2 The red–blue continuum

The majority of respondents profess themselves to be moderate red or moderate blue. Some explain their choice with statements like 'It depends on the situation' or 'I am red in my work role and blue at home' (and vice versa). That is OK. The continuum attempts to link the concepts of red and blue to your self-assessment.

As I shall show, neither all red nor all blue is the most effective negotiating outlook. Even alternating between red and blue is defective. But before we discuss a viable alternative strategy, we have much more work to do.

For your toolkit

T3.1 Avoid the temptation to win at somebody else's expense.

T3.2 Do not interrupt someone, even if they are clearly factually incorrect; however, if somebody interrupts you, give way.

T3.3 Always try to negotiate even if the other party appears 'unreasonable'.

T3.4 Refrain from walking out of negotiations – and if you must terminate a negotiation abruptly, always state the time and place for resuming.

T3.5 Do not accept as final that something is 'non-negotiable' merely by the other party's declaration, but nevertheless treat the issue and their defensiveness with respect.

T3.6 Identify 'red' attitudes as a determination to ensure that 'more for me means less for you'.

T3.7 Identify 'blue' attitudes as the acceptance that 'less for me is OK'.

Chapter 4
What drives your behaviour?

➡ THE SEQUENCE

The beauty of classifying negotiating attitudes as red and blue is that we can use the same labels to classify the negotiating behaviours associated with the attitudes. Thus, a person with red attitudes usually, but not always, exhibits red behaviours.

Fortunately you do not have to identify their attitudes before you can identify their likely behaviours, because in practice you observe their behaviour first, from which you may infer their attitudes. This sequence has the advantage, whatever their protestations to the contrary or the plausibility of their persuasion, that the superior evidence of their behaviour is the safest (for you) indicator of their intentions.

It is how negotiators *behave* that is decisive. You cannot, nor do you need, to see into their heads nor tap into their thoughts. Their behaviour is visible and audible. Simply watch and listen. You observe how they behave and you interpret your observation. Thus, the first step towards enhancing your negotiating performance is to observe the evidence of people's behaviour.

➡ YOUR ATTITUDES BECOME YOUR BEHAVIOUR

How do red and blue attitudes manifest themselves as red and blue behaviours?

The demeanour of red negotiators usually is openly domineering, though you should be careful, in the absence of an openly domineering style, of jumping to rash conclusions that they are not red negotiators for two good reasons. First, their apparent aggressive stance could be the result of their recoil from previous provocation by you or your associates: ruin somebody's holiday arrangements and you cannot expect them to be timid in expressing their feelings. Secondly, some red players project nothing but disarming charm, even sweetness and light, while doggedly pursuing their intentions of acquiring most of what is on the table. Used car sellers, double glazing 'consultants' and estate agents have all excelled in acquiring reputations for deviousness. They are some of the 'devious' reds compared with the more visible 'open' reds.

The behaviour of blue negotiators usually is visibly submissive, though again you should be careful not to judge too hastily. Some people are naturally self-effacing and, behind their politeness and their softly expressed inter-personal skills, there is a hard core of determination that belies their appearance of being a push-over. Many blues are indeed pushed-over by little more than a gentle prod. They don't say 'boo' to a goose because they genuinely fear the goose's retaliatory squawk.

Try not to let my caveats undermine your enthusiasm for the red and blue distinction. The good news is that you have more than one test for behavioural intentions and need not rely on first impressions. The likelihood of adopting misleading impressions from observing initial behaviour should come as no surprise. Devious people, who write their scripts, mouth their lines and carefully censor their messages, put on a favourable act deliberately to mislead you.

Activity 4.1

Now be honest. Think of an occasion on which you recently put on an act about how you felt, while inside you were boiling with rage. It might have been with your relatives (or your partner's), your neighbour, your boss, your boss's boss, the driver of another car, or the police officer who stopped you. Just think of the incident and what specifically you said and how you said it (ignore judgemental urges).

Activity 4.1 introduces the content of a negotiator's behaviour as distinct from its form. The content is the message, while the form is the way it is delivered. The two forms of aggressive and passive behaviour can also deliver the same message: you may aggressively require someone to restore your just deserts or you may passively relieve them of your entitlement. Therefore, to get a fix on what a negotiator is about, you need to assess the behavioural form *and* its content.

➡ TAKERS AND GIVERS

Here I introduce you to two of the main contents of negotiation behaviour, namely, 'taking' and 'giving'. These classifications conveniently correspond to the red and blue colours of behaviour.

Content classified as 'taking' is the set of behaviours that serve the purpose of red players, who try to take from the transaction their wants at the expense, or in disregard, of your wants. Red takers make demands without offers:

> We demand higher wages for pilots and, as you can't fly planes without pilots, your planes won't fly from Tuesday unless we get our money.

> Look, if you want to remain in my property you will pay my rent increase, otherwise Claude and Henri here will introduce you and your furniture to the street.

> This is how it is in this Mission: if you're here, then you sing His hymns. Got it?

Red players reveal their intentions in both the form and the content of their messages.

Activity 4.2

When was the last time you made a 'red' demand? Can you recollect the exact words you used? Think about why you thought it appropriate to make a red demand on that occasion.

Content classified as 'giving', on the other hand, is the mirror image of red behaviour. It covers the set of behaviours that serves the purpose of blue players. You give to the other negotiator what they want at the expense, or in disregard of, your own wants.

Red players intimidate blue players into conceding to the redder player, but blue players also concede of their own volition without intimidation. Blue players want to 'give' because they see their (often illusory) relationship with the taking party as more important than the result. Parenting, for example, is often accompanied by blue behaviour towards the children.

Giving someone what they want makes blue players feel good about themselves. Refraining from driving a hard bargain causes them no great material or psychic loss, because their behaviour conforms to their blue attitudes. Even an appropriate bargain – one commensurate with what they are giving – may have no attraction for them as a result. It is just not in their attitudinal make-up to be one of nature's takers.

Blue givers make offers without demands:

> We understand your concerns with costs, profits and performance and we certainly empathise with your problems. We will co-operate by not pressing for higher wages for pilots because of the financial situation. Meanwhile, we will happily continue to fly the planes.

> Look, as my landlord if you want to increase my rent that is your privilege, as it is a great privilege for me to stay here. Would you, Mr. Claude and Mr. Henri care to join me in a beer?

> OK, this is the Lord's Mission and I'd love to sing His hymns. Which one shall I sing first?

Activity 4.3

When did you last make a 'blue' offer? What circumstances made you do so? Were you intimidated and not sure what else you could do? Or is 'giving' your natural inclination?

➡ **MIXTURES OF RED AND BLUE**

So far I have presented you with only two options, red or blue. If you remained trapped between only choosing one or the other, then fruitful negotiation would indeed be a mirage, neither within your reach nor your grasp. But before I solve that dilemma, it is essential that you recognise 'red' and 'blue' as the most common behavioural traits in untrained negotiators.

While not many negotiators remain irreversibly stuck in either a red or blue mode for all their negotiations, you occasionally come across them. They find, presumably, it congenial to their inclinations to be monchromatic. If they come across a redder or bluer player than themselves, they might be uncomfortable, but not for long. Extreme reds eventually run out of blue submissives to bully and extreme blues run out of resources to give away.

Most untrained negotiators oscillate between red and blue behaviours, often within the same negotiating sequence with the same person. Without realising it, they switch between demanding and offering one-way deals.

Activity 4.4

Think of a recent experience in which you behaved sometimes red and sometimes blue. Can you remember why you behaved this way?

From many observations, I conclude that most negotiators mix red and blue behaviours. They break each negotiating move into small steps, in some of which they behave in a red (taking) manner and others in a blue (giving) manner. Fortunately for business success, their negotiating ploys eventually emerge into a mutually acceptable agreement.

Trillions of negotiations take place across the planet every year, and more will continue to do so because the growth in world trade is truly staggering. In addition, there are changes in family relationships, organisational norms and political practice, all of which support the growth of the negotiating method. This means that billions of negotiations successfully conclude every day and so, despite my allegation that most people are not good at negotiating (any more than they are good at sex!), many hundreds of millions of people do it well enough to achieve acceptable results.

It is good to remember this in case you believe that negotiating is too difficult or too diffuse for you to grasp. Understanding the complexities of negotiation is well within the reach of the overwhelming majority of people. To benefit, you only need some behavioural tools and plenty of opportunities to practise using them.

For your toolkit

T4.1 Identify as 'red' any behaviour that seeks to take without giving.

T4.2 Identify as 'blue' any behaviour that seeks to give without taking.

T4.3 Rely solely on other negotiators' behaviour as indicators of their intentions, and not on their verbal affirmations about their intentions.

T4.4 Identify the colour of negotiators' attitudes from the colour of their behaviour.

T4.5 Because most people mix their behaviours between red and blue, avoid too hasty a conclusion about their intentions from a single behaviour.

Chapter 5
Decisions, Decisions

➡ ON LISTS

Management trainers love labels, and they become ecstatic if their labels form a neat list.

Activity 5.1

Have you noticed how trainers fill flip charts and OHP slides with lists and distribute hand-outs full of lists? Why do you think they do this?

Lists jog jaded memories and lend coherence to lectures. Also, for the lazy or incompetent trainer, a list saves on preparation time, especially if it is cribbed from a colleague or copied from a book. Classification is the elementary beginning of scientific enquiry. In botany, classification is an obsession. In astronomy, the list of star names is so long – and recent names so obscure – that numbers now dominate star maps as identifiers.

The universal body of knowledge (the ultimate product of social evolution) requires stable classifications, and sometimes strict taxonomies too. This is not always possible. With the end of colonialism and communism, place names changed around the world (sometimes two or three times). Changing place names is only mildly and temporarily confusing, but the consequence, say, of changing the meridians of longitude to suit political agendas, or of recasting all the Latin names for plant life into Arabic or Chinese, hardly bears contemplation.

So while the benefit of imposing a system of classification on disparate data is often worthy of the effort, classification of decision making need only be as crude as mere labelling. The diseconomies, however, of too strict a labelling of decision making are twofold.

First, the arbitrariness of labelling, say, one decision-making mode as 'pure negotiation' and another as 'pure persuasion' impedes understanding when the minute gradations between 'negotiation' and 'persuasion' are important. A label strictly separating closely related phenomena, such as negotiation and persuasion, downgrades the value of those cases that consist of neither pure negotiation nor pure persuasion but various shades of both.

Secondly, even the crude labels attached to phenomena sometimes become stale through repetition, and they lose their richness. It is too easy to forget the meaningful distinctions between, and similarities of, related phenomena, and rattle through lists of labels as a mere chore, which it is for a trainer struggling to deliver 'once more with feeling' her n-thousandth exposition of overused labels.

➡ FORMS OF DECISION MAKING

The differences between negotiation and other forms of decision making in the context of red and blue behaviours illustrate my assertions. It is fashionable to identify negotiation as one of several forms of decision making and to list it as different from others. On this occasion, I present the distinctions between these decision-making forms in a manner different from usual treatments.

The labels for the other forms include: persuade, instruct, coerce, submit, arbitrate, chance (as in 'toss a coin'), postpone, vote, consensus, reject, and problem solve. These alternatives differ from negotiation to varying degrees. At the same time, they all also have important affinities with negotiation. You should examine and understand their affinities rather than merely rush through their differences.

Remember, red and blue attitudes dominate all decision-making behaviours and not just negotiation, and at any moment you are either in one colour mode or the other.

Persuasion

Take the decision-making mode of 'persuasion'. This differs from negotiation because it does not require an explicit exchange of something for something. You persuade another party to do something by virtue of, say, your argument and reason (which, incidentally, are two more labels!).

Activity 5.2

In this first cut at the differences, can you see potential traces of the colours of behaviour in the activity of persuasion?

Argument can vary in degree from the clear statement of a case through to an abrasive verbal altercation. Your argument, if based on red premises, leads to red conclusions ('all foreigners are untrustworthy; Pedro is a foreigner, therefore Pedro is untrustworthy'). If you accept the (false) premise, the false (red) conclusion follows.

You can raise the temperature of your argument by your tone and supporting allegations. You could elaborate on features of Pedro's antecedents, the country he comes from, a list of his alleged misdemeanours, and ascribe to him motives that support your arguments. This suggests that argument leans to the red end of the persuasion continuum.

The use of reason (or your version of it) leans to the blue end of the persuasion continuum. Your premise may not be so obviously flawed as the argument supporting the alleged untrustworthiness of Pedro. You may use genuine supporting evidence, carefully mustered and elaborated upon, and appeal to the likelihood of the truth of what you allege, based on your character or the characters of your witnesses. Once convinced by persuasion, you suppress incredulity.

If your antagonists answer credibly every argument you muster against their persuasion, your resistance wanes. If you fight – justifiably or from ignorance – against their persuasive pressure, then your emotions change in tone from rational discourse towards heated argument.

The first conclusion to glean from this example is that red and blue behaviours are not specific to any mode of decision making. It is as if you were on a tightrope; a slight shift in balance and you tip to your red side; a slight shift the other way and you tip to your blue side. Both colours of behaviour easily dominate your mind and are ever present.

And that tightrope image is important to recall when negotiating. The human behaviours of both red and blue have a history as long as that of our species, and I have observed in practice that all present day decision-making modes can generate both red or blue behaviour. Sure, I can list (with apologies!) conventionally labelled decision-making behaviours as either red or blue, as in Figure 5.1, but you may equally well reverse the lists under the columns!

Red	Blue
Coercion	Persuasion
Instruct	Arbitrate
Reject	Postpone
Chance	Consensus
Vote	Submit
	Problem solve

Figure 5.1 Conventional categories of decision making

Activity 5.3

Do you see how seductive list-making becomes? Review the importance (or otherwise) of categorising items in your own experience.

I have shown the red and blue sides of persuasion, itself conventionally classified as blue. Now each side of red and blue can separate again. You can have blue argument (a mathematical function that submits without fuss to the data) and you can have red rationality (Adolph Hitler's case against the Versailles Peace Treaty in *Mein Kampf*).

Activity 5.4

To which decision mode might the line, 'Make him an offer he can't refuse' belong?

Furthermore, you can have red coercion (Serbian thugs beating up Albanians) and blue coercion (enforcing the submission of everybody to drive in the same direction on the same side of the road). You can have red consensus (a jury proclaiming an innocent person guilty) and blue consensus (no persecuted minorities). You can have red voting (discrimination against a minority) and blue voting (an exhaustive ballot to elect the least-disliked candidate). And so on.

Activity 5.5

Make notes on red and blue examples in the decison-making mode 'instruction'.

Also try the same exercise with the decision-making mode 'arbitration'. (Hint. Think of the colours of the applicable rules and the outcome.)

Now try finding examples of red and blue in the decision-making mode: 'problem solve'. (Hint: think of differences between voluntary and compulsory problem solving.)

➡ MIXTURES OF DECISION-MAKING FORMS

What is true for alternative forms of decision making individually is also true when they combine and interact within the same process. No negotiation, for example, totally isolates itself from incursions and interventions from other decision-making forms. They are freely introduced by the participants and there is not much others can do to stop this.

There is thus no 'pure' negotiation process, except for the most trivial or singular 'bid and accept or reject' instant trades practised in foreign-exchange dealing. To flirt with the notion that a single decision-making process operates entirely on its own is naïve and impracticable. In all forms of decision making, you interact with, and draw upon the skills and behaviours of, other methods.

Nobody, for instance, woke up one day aeons ago and decided for the first time ever to negotiate. There was no primeval first negotiator in our species – nor for that matter was there a first persuader or a first bully. Behavioural adaptations tend to build on earlier minute and cumulated experiments – some that work and others that fail – just as knowledge builds on cumulated sequences of conjectures and refutations. The evidence for this assertion is in your own behaviour.

Activity 5.6

Do you compartmentalise yourself into negotiating modes, per-suading modes, gambling modes, and such like? Consider your approach to decision making, and whether it is 'pure' or a mixture.

As a child you fawned, cried, leapt into tantrums, sought favour, did favours, made happy faces, shed tears, and generally did anything to get what you momentarily wanted, and you let adults know how you felt when they didn't oblige. There is no sharp dividing line between the parade of methods you chose as a child and those you practise when you make decisions as an adult. In the common discourse of negotiation, you use persuasion of both red and blue hues to suit the circumstances and the reaction of the other person. The melding of persuasion skills with negotiating behaviours helps you if the other party is receptive to your persuasion.

Indeed, you might open with persuasion with the intention of getting what you want by that means alone, and then find it doesn't work. Instead of the other party unilaterally giving you what you want, they might make it clear that if they are to comply with your wishes they expect something more from you than fine words and rational arguments. Suddenly, you do not have a singular persuasion process to work through but must contemplate trying something else to achieve what persuasion alone failed to deliver. And even then there is no guarantee that your first resort will be to negotiation, or that they will be receptive to your attempts to switch to another method of finding a solution.

Activity 5.7

When did you last face a difficulty in persuading someone to do something? Did you switch to negotiation or to something else?

Coercion

If persuasion fails, evidence suggests that most people slip into some degree of coercive behaviour, usually of a red hue, ranging from sulking through to threatening. 'No more Mr Nice Guy' becomes the mood. From friendly persuasion to ugly retribution, it takes only a short shift in your balance on the behavioural tightrope.

But how different is coercion from persuasion? Could it be merely a different form of persuasion, and cannot persuasion be seen as merely a different form of coercion? As always, it depends on your terms and their context and from which side of the transaction you take your perspective.

A blue negotiator, subjected to a quietly presented summary of the likely course of events if they resist the redder player, might feel they had no option but to submit. They could feel (were?) coercively persuaded or persuasively coerced! Another negotiator, subjected to fiercely presented threats of the consequences of not complying with a red demand, might with justice feel brutally coerced into complying. It all depends on context.

King Charles I, when arrested by a young Cromwellian cavalry officer (and only a lowly Cornet to boot!), asked to see the written 'Commission' that gave the young man the right to arrest his King. The young officer pointed to the squadron of armed cavalry mounted behind him, to which King Charles commented, wryly, 'And what a fine Commission you have too'. At least he had a sense of humour.

For your toolkit

T5.1 Use lists of attributes from two perspectives: as fine distinctions and as shades with similarities.

T5.2 Remember, all decision-making forms can be either red or blue in behaviour.

T5.3 Instruction may be red ('Do this or else!') or blue ('Take the day off').

T5.4 Problem solving may be red ('I won't contemplate any other method') or blue ('Let us try solving this problem').

T5.5 You can mix decision-making methods together.

T5.6 You may mix non-argumentative persuasion behaviours with negotiating.

T5.7 Refrain from mixing coercive behaviours with negotiating, but in some contexts red coercion may be a heavy form of blue persuasion.

T5.8 Think of negotiating as balancing on a tightrope while you switch between red and blue.

Chapter 6
Risking trust

➡ WHY PLAY RED?

Intuitively, most people consider that red behaviour is contrary to socially approved behaviour, and dubious in manner, so why do decision makers play red? A good question because it goes to the heart of the problem of interactive behaviour. I will answer it and then suggest some tools for dealing with red behaviour when it comes – as it surely will – across your negotiating table.

What is the problem confronting every individual when they interact with another individual? In one word: trust, the self-certificated virtue! Everybody claims to be trustworthy, and they do so with an indignation that tolerates no doubts, but nobody can ever be sure that anybody else can be trusted.

Yet trust is the linchpin of interactive behaviour and doubts about trust make interacting risky. Without trust, so much of what we gain to our great benefit from interacting would not – could not – happen. We inherit an instinct for distrust, and we learn to distinguish between when it is safe to overcome our instinct and when it is safer to follow it.

➡ JAKE'S PARABLE ON TRUST

Let us consider a simple parable about trust. The setting may be unusual, the players unattractive, and their dilemma one you would avoid, but if you can learn about the trust problem from a parable, what is the harm?

Jake is on a business trip to Ogoland, a once-prosperous oil-rich country ravaged by the stupid economic policies of its President, who treats the Public Treasury as his private bank account. Hence the national currency, the quonk, is not worth much and it costs many of Jake's dollars in exchange for enough quonks to buy a glass of the local beer. Indeed, yesterday $100 bought Jake only Q20, and last evening it cost Q5 to buy him a glass of warm beer. By all accounts, beer at $25 a small glass is expensive.

Tonight, a man somewhat furtively approaches Jake and offers him a deal:

'I will give you Q200 for your $100,' says the man. 'Interested?'

'Sure,' says Jake, never one to miss a business opportunity.

'Good,' says the man, adding, 'There is only one problem. In Ogoland it is very dangerous to be caught changing currency unofficially. Our President's nephew runs the state bank and he doesn't like competition. His secret police are everywhere.'

'Damn it,' says Jake, who had already calculated that the man's exchange rate would bring his beer price down from $25 to $2.50, which was a wholly more satisfying price for quenching his thirst.

'I have a cunning plan,' says the man.

'Great,' enthuses Jake.

'You see yonder park bench over there?' says the man. 'Well, you take your $100 and wrap it in this envelope and leave it under the bench. Meanwhile, I'll take my Q200 notes in this envelope and leave it under the pillow in your room. Then we swap places and as we can't get caught by the secret police we both live happily ever after.'

'Wow,' exclaims Jake, 'what a brilliant plan. OK, let's do it.'

After shaking hands to seal their agreement, they separate and go to complete their business.

Activity 6.1

What do you think of the plan? Can you spot any flaws in it? (Ignore legalities.)

The best laid schemes

If the plan works, the man ends up with scarce foreign dollars that are worth a lot more than Q20 on the informal market, and Jake ends up with realistically priced local beer and perhaps even a clean glass, if he tips generously.

But Burns' lines about 'the best laid plans o' mice an' men' spring to mind (i.e., those that 'gang aft a-gley'). And 'a-gley' this plan looks likely to go. Why? Because of nagging doubts about trust, and where trust is in doubt you behave accordingly.

Activity 6.2

Assume Jake has doubts once he sets off for the park bench. He may fully intend to put the envelope with his $100 in it under the bench, but will he?

What might go through his mind? What would go through your mind if offered the same deal?

Can Jake trust the stranger to carry out his side of the bargain? If Jake trusts the man to put Q200 under his pillow and the man doesn't, Jake could end up $100 poorer and without the benefit of cheaper beer. Once the man is out of sight, who knows what he might do? He could place a torn-up newspaper under the pillow, or not even bother to go to Jake's room. All he has to do is wait until Jake leaves his $100 under the park bench, cross the road, pick up Jake's money and scarper.

Activity 6.3

Assume the man has doubts once he leaves Jake and sets off for Jake's room. He may fully intend to put the envelope with his Q200 in it under the pillow, but will he?

What might go through his mind? What would go through your mind?

Can the man trust Jake to carry out *his* side of the bargain? Once Jake is out of sight, who knows what he might do? He could leave an envelope stuffed with old menus under the park bench. All Jake has to do is wait until the man leaves the Q200 under the pillow, then go upstairs to pocket the man's money and head for the bar.

The frailty of trust

So, a workable plan, of benefit to both of them if they carry it out, is in jeopardy because they lack trust. It's no good insisting that for the plan to work they should trust each other and act like 'gentlemen'. The word 'trust' has different connotations to the words 'blind faith'. Both Jake and the money changer can only know what they themselves will do, but neither can know for certain what the other will do.

Just because you wish them to be trustworthy, or, in that final illusion of the naïve, just because you *act* as if they are trustworthy, your wish or illusion is no guarantee against disappointment. To the degree to which you recognise these sentiments, to that degree you understand the dilemma of trust.

Activity 6.4

How would you classify the behaviours that Jake and the money changer can demonstrate?

Is the act of them leaving the money as agreed a blue or red behaviour? Is the act of them not leaving the money as agreed blue or red?

Jake and the man have two options: to *co-operate* and place their money as agreed; or to *defect* and withhold their money. Though co-operation is analogous to blue behaviour and defection to red behaviour, I hesitate to use analogies that carry normative baggage such as: 'co-operation is good; defection is bad'. Casual labelling of behaviour often leads to moral pressure to behave in one way and eschew another. That does not mean that moral persuasion is effective.

Because exhortation works less effectively than self-interest, moral pressure is less effective. This never prevents governments from spending millions on exhortation campaigns, which seldom achieve anything except the ends of those who sell exhortation campaigns to gullible governments.

Some people have mistaken the lessons from Jake's dilemma, showing how easy it is to misunderstand what should be clear. They mistakenly recast the dilemma of trust into a lesson about moral goodness. Jake's problem is not one of a lack of moral fibre; nor, necessarily, is it wrong for him to defect.

Costs and benefits of defection

Let's be risqué and ask: how should Jake calculate the costs and benefits to him of his choices? I know some people think material calculation is inappropriate in what they see as a moral issue, but bear with me.

If both Jake and the money changer complete their commitments, then Jake is better off by Q200 (ignore the official rate) and the money changer is better off by $100. Now, if Jake defects but the money changer doesn't, Jake is unambiguously better off because he ends up with the money changer's Q200 and keeps his $100. Meanwhile, the money changer is unambiguously worse off because he loses his Q200 and doesn't get Jake's $100. Conversely, if the money changer defects and Jake doesn't, then the money changer is unambiguously better off because he gains Jake's $100 and keeps his Q200. Meanwhile, Jake is unambiguously worse off because he loses his $100 and doesn't gain the money changer's Q200. This only leaves one other outcome: both Jake and the money changer defect, so that neither gains and neither loses (except they lose the opportunity to be better off if they had both co-operated).

Now compare the possible outcomes and see how they guide Jake's behaviour (and, by inference, the behaviour of the money changer). The outcomes of either joint co-operation and joint defection are a joint gain or the avoidance of a joint loss.

Activity 6.5

Why, in the conditions just specified, is it rational for Jake to defect?

The risk of losing from a failed joint co-operation is very high for a co-operator who deals with a defector. If Jake co-operates and the money changer defects, Jake loses his $100. Jake only avoids the loss of $100 by either co-operating with a co-operator or defecting. But Jake also gains as a defector if the money changer co-operates, because then he keeps his $100 and gains Q200.

As Jake does not, and cannot, know in advance whether the money changer is a co-operator or a defector, it pays him to defect in case the money changer is a defector. Jake keeps his $100, and, if the money changer is a co-operator, it doubly pays Jake to defect because he keeps the money changer's Q200 as well.

Activity 6.6

What is the rational decision for the money changer?

What is true for Jake is also true for the money changer. Hence, the rewards of distrust drives them both to defect and, because whoever defects when the other co-operates gains, the most likely outcome is a double defection. Therefore the money changer's plan is flawed.

➡ MOTIVES AND INTENTIONS

Before you commit the error of totally recasting Jake's parable as a morality tale and, by implication, lamenting his materialism and castigating the alleged pernicious role of distrust, consider the consequences that so far I have ignored.

I usually separate behaviour from motives and intentions, mainly to avoid straying into moral philosophy. In this case, consideration of possible motives is admissible because I have already alluded to them in the choice between defection and co-operation. Risk is the obverse of trust – you can't have one without the other. In choosing a behaviour, the risks of the choices intrude on the chooser. If you want to eliminate risk, you must eliminate trust (as any security officer will tell you).

What might motivate Jake's choice? I pick two possible motives. First, he can choose to defect because co-operation exposes him to the risk of losing $100 if the money changer defects. Call this a *motive to protect* himself (and his $100). Alternatively, he can

choose to defect because he anticipates that the money changer
will co-operate and by defecting he gains Q200. Call this a *motive to
exploit* a co-operator.

Of these twin motives, to protect one's self or to exploit another,
which one motivates Jake when he defects?

While Jake knows which of these motives drives his behaviour,
the money changer does not and cannot know what motivates
Jake. Again, he is at that first and final frontier: he can't see inside
another person's mind. And hence, while I acknowledge the
importance of motivation in driving behaviour (I am not so
extreme a behaviourist as to deny the relevance of motives), I also
insist that another person's motivation is not accessible to
anybody but that person.

You cannot rely on affirmations of what motivates a person, so
you must rely on their behaviour – but their behaviour can have
multiple motivations. We seem trapped when we try to fathom
motives and intentions.

➡ INSTINCTS OF SELF-PRESERVATION

To escape from the trap, follow your instincts.

No, I don't mean by this an exhortation to follow your 'gut
instincts' (whatever they are) about someone. Blind trust involves
moral judgements and has high attendant risks. For Jake an error
of judgement only costs $100. In some circumstances, misjudging
someone's motives could cost your life. I am referring to your
inherited instincts of self-preservation. They are reliable, in the
strict sense that they are safe. You inherited them from your
ancestors, whose redeeming qualities, whatever their morals, was
their success at living long enough to breed, which is why you are
alive to read this advice. The brutal course of events culled those
with inadequate instincts for self-preservation and ensured (unintentionally) that these people didn't succeed, while our ancestors
did.

So apply your inheritance to the problem: how do you know what motivates another's behaviour towards you? Unable to know what motivates them, apply the instinctive rule: ascribe to them the motives that are safest for your survival. In short: assume the worst will happen and behave accordingly.

Activity 6.8

Can you see the behavioural consequence of each of Jake and the money changer acting to counter the worst motives they can ascribe to the other? Does it matter whether the ascribed motives are true?

The worst motive, in Jake's context, is that the money changer intends to exploit him. To co-operate in this circumstance exposes Jake to exploitation and he protects himself best by not leaving his $100 under the park bench. Of course, the money changer does not know what Jake will do but, reasoning analogously, he must assume that Jake will exploit him and, therefore, to protect himself he must defect too. It is credible to believe that both Jake and the money changer defect to protect themselves and not intentionally to exploit the other. It is also credible to believe that they both defect to exploit each other and not solely to protect themselves. Or even that one defects to protect and the other to exploit.

In behavioural terms the consequences of ascribing to them their motivations amounts to the same thing: by defecting, they survive to play other games (and so do their descendants). The truth of the ascription of the worst motive to them, therefore, is irrelevant.

Social evolution, fast as it is compared with biological evolution, still took a long time before people found ways to ensure trust in their interactions. For thousands of years it was safer to stay distant from other human groups and, if contact was unavoidable, to assume the worst about their intentions and kill them before they killed you (nowadays in sport it is called 'getting your retaliation in first'). Warfare, cruelty and so-called 'senseless' violence have major roles in those primitive societies that we know about and, by inference, the same features presumably had similar roles in those societies that preceded them.

That is why remnants of this 'safer' behaviour reappear as the red–blue dilemma in negotiation and in other forms of decision making. That is why someone's red behaviour in negotiation is not a character defect, nor something that can be 'cured' by acquired morality.

Jake is perfectly sensible to behave the way he does. It you asked him why he defected, he wouldn't need a PhD in behavioural psychology to reply: 'I behave as a defector in those circumstances not because I want to but because I must.'

➡ CO-OPERATIVE TRAITS

Some people, as noted, become depressed when they contemplate the red–blue dilemma. They jump to the fallacious conclusion that Jake's parable is a nihilist testament against trust and co-operation. If blue naiveté is inevitably self destructive and red aggressiveness is morally disturbing, what is there left for ethical people? Is it a case for Matthew Arnold's pessimism: 'Madman or slave, must man be one?'

Not at all. Books, necessarily are written (and read) in a linear format and you cannot cover all parts of an argument simultaneously! It is essential that you first understand the red–blue dilemma before you appreciate how the solution is constructed. This we shall now do in general before picking it up again 'in praise of purple' in Chapter 12.

Red, as in 'red in tooth and claw', is only one snapshot of the human heritage – our animal side, so to speak. It is not the final word about our humanity, though plenty of humans over the millennia have behaved as if that is all our species is about. Popular presentations of human relationships sometimes fixate on images of violence as if non-violence is an aberration.

A recent article of mine on red–blue behaviours was illustrated by a coloured photograph of a savage dog in a wide-jawed aggressive fighting pose. Somehow the academic editor missed my point. The notion that savagery is our historical inheritance and that co-operative behaviour is a manifestation of our civilised values is totally false. Humans are capable of both appalling savagery (Bosnia, Rwanda and Northern Ireland, are but a few recent examples) and also enlightened co-operation. The truth is that for as long as humans were evolving as a distinct species, we have been capable of both sets of behaviours. Co-operation (speaking generically) is not a product of civilisation, as some imagine it to be. It is as much a part of our inheritance as is our being, on occasion, 'red in tooth and claw' – did not the gentle Jesus whip the money changers out of the Temple?

Some animals engage in behaviour towards members of their own species in a quasi-altruistic manner (for example, vampire bats share blood and chimpanzees show solidarity in fights). In humans, this behaviour is so well documented as to be beyond controversy. But why should co-operation have become so highly developed in humans compared with other animals, and how did it become an active defining trait?

Consider the nature of an advantage, amongst our ancestors, such as a tendency to co-operate. Hunters were puny compared to their prey, but by combining they could make bigger kills, or if they found a recently dead large animal, by combining to eat it they would physically strengthen their band of around forty individuals – and one result would be that more of the band's children would survive to have children.

No individual could physically consume an entire animal and much would be wasted if he only ate his fill and left the rest to rot, but by sharing the animal within the band, the bodies of the satiated band stored the animal as effectively as a refrigerator. True, the sharers did not have access to the consumed meat in the bodies of the band (they were not cannibals), but they did have access to the kills of other members of the band when they made them or found them.

Thus, an individual co-operator sharing with other co-operators could prosper in the sense that a reproductive advantage would develop over bands with no co-operators in them, or with subuded proclivities to co-operate, or with too many defectors.

People living in extendable families within hunting bands did not face Jake's dilemma of a one-hit decision: co-operate or defect. They had a constant flow of repetitive games to repeat the decision–choice over and over again with people they knew intimately. And within those games, reciprocation was essential for the benefits of co-operation to exceed the costs. If you shared and others didn't, you lost out – perhaps fatally.

In co-operative reciprocation, the exchange is implicit, separated in time and only probable, not certain: the other party may defect on their obligation. In negotiation, the exchange is explicit ('If you give me this, then I will give you that'). The negotiated exchange is simultaneous, conditional and contingent. In this way cheaters are spotted almost immediately, because they do not exchange what they agreed and the deficit is very visible and immediate.

Activity 6.9

Have you ever done somebody a specific favour, or put yourself out for them in some significant way, and then, later, when you need them to do you a favour of a similar, or lesser, magnitude, they fail to do so without in your view any good reason? They just don't reciprocate.

How did you react to this situation? Were you annoyed? Does it still rankle?

Defectors are punished, if not immediately, certainly when they try to treat for another exchange. The ostracism they face from former co-operators who refuse to co-operate with them again is total, specific and unremitting. This is especially so if they are members of the same band. Either they withdraw from the band and form their own, or they perish in their isolation.

Do not underestimate the fine calculus of who owed what to whom that reciprocal co-operation induced in the mindsets of the hunter–gatherers, and do not misjudge the extent to which that mental apparatus has been passed to you. Constant interaction within small bands of hunter–gatherers refined the ability to spot defectors. When Jake engages in dialogue about a possible currency deal with the money changer (a total stranger), his suspicions about possible cheating are not something he picked up from exposure to modern culture or from his neglect of classes in religious morality; it is something in his inherited psyche that came to him courtesy of his ancestors.

A defector reaps the benefit of co-operation without contributing to the cost. It is a short-term advantage because, once spotted,
the opportunities for defection in subsequent transactions are
limited. In fact, being a stranger or an unknown party, suspicions
about being a possible defector become prominent, which inhibits
co-operation.

➡ TIT-FOR-TAT

The co-operator does best who operates according to the rule given
by: open a transaction of any kind with another person with a co-
operative move and then react according to how the other party
reacts.

If the other party reciprocates in co-operation – i.e. they return
the favour or complete the bargain – then the co-operator
continues to co-operate. But if the other party defects, then the co-
operator withdraws from co-operation and (effectively) defects in
retaliation. This is known as a 'tit-for-tat' strategy.

Put succinctly in our red–blue analogy, the behaviour is to play
blue on the first move and then do whatever the other party does
in response. If they play red to your blue, play red back on the
subsequent move; if they play blue, you play blue and continue to
do so until they defect. The constraint on a co-operator is never to
initiate red play and always to respond to blue play with instant
blue play, no matter how long the run of red play.

In computer experiments applying this rule, it was found that
tit-for-tat programs did better than all other programs when
played against all others. Thus, although some defection strategies
did well enough against tit-for-tat (they struck it lucky and made
heavy gains in some circumstances), when they were played across
all the strategies in repetitive games they lost out. Meanwhile, tit-
for-tat, which lost against some individual plays (who struck it
lucky) gained heavily on sufficient occasions to pile up high
positive scores. The conclusion is inescapable: co-operation is a
robust strategy.

Unintentionally, the gains to the group as a whole are found to
exceed by a wide margin the losses from acts of altruism to any one

individual. Therefore, defecting to exploit somebody's co-operation might create enormous gains to a single defector but the
short-term benefit of a defecting strategy is insignificant compared
with the gains of group co-operation.

In Jake's case, suppose the money changer defects. What would
you expect Jake to do if the money changer reappeared, apologised
and offered to complete the transaction a second time?

If you think Jake would give him another chance (unlikely in my
view) and the money changer defects again, would you expect Jake
to give him a third or fourth chance?

As long as individuals can identify defectors or cease transacting
with those who defect but continue co-operating with co-operators, co-operation benefits those who co-operate and, by exten-
sion, benefits the group. There are a myriad of transactions
possible each day in even a small group. Few single transactions are
a life or death decision, so defection is not decisive. But as long as
the punishment for defection – withdrawal of co-operation – is
certain, defection cannot prosper.

Modern hunter–gatherers in simplistic societies demonstrate a
capacity for spotting and punishing cheats, using varying degrees
of ostracism. But so do modern families, work groups and
organisations, although the margin of survival in our modern
world is much wider than it was in the Pleistocene era, and the
punishment of defection is less draconian.

Activity 6.11 requires you to examine the tensions in your
family, but if you examine any extended family you will find,
within the interpersonal grumbles, evidence for the assertion that
– at bottom – these tensions relate to instances of defection.

Examine your own extended family and, if it is fairly normal, there
will be at least one relative with whom you do not get along as well
as the others in the family group. Why is this?

What did that person do to cause the offence of which they are accused? Is it an example of your identification of a 'defector' of some kind?

Check out some friends and ask them about potential defectors among their relatives.

Get closer to your work group and try to explain why you get on better with some of them than others. Is there a trace of suspected or actual defection in these cases?

➡ SOLVING THE DILEMMA OF TRUST

The world is not ruled entirely by the red–blue dilemma. These attitudes and their attendant behaviours are extremely common (probably with red behaviour a majority trait) but co-operative behaviour is also well represented in all cultures. Interpersonal interactions are so numerous and segmented that no single defection in normal circumstances totally destroys everything a person has or wants. All the eggs are seldom in one basket – if they are, keep your eye on the basket!

The co-operative mechanism appears to have been ever-present, and centuries of tyranny have not obliterated it. Friendships form even in the most distressing of circumstances as well as those within which it is safe to transact. Informal co-operation operates at all levels of society, irrespective of the prevailing ideology. True, it took many millennia for the seed of trust we call 'trade' to flower, but it would be wrong to ignore its deep roots in the history of our species.

That is what brings you to the solution to the dilemma of trust. In two areas – explicit negotiation and implicit reciprocation, or influence – you solve the dilemma almost daily, if not hourly. You transact with others because it is in your nature to do so. You identify cheats and likely cheats (the money changer) and avoid them before you become a victim, or, if it is too late and you are a victim, you avoid them in future. And the good news is that, in general, the gains from your successful attempts at co-operation exceed the losses from the occasional defection.

Now that you (hopefully) understand a common aspect of negotiating behaviour better than you did, you can build behavioural tools that help you to resolve the dilemma of the risk of trust and that thereby help you to benefit from interactive interdependence on others. What seems to be random and inexplicable behaviour now has meaning, and the best way to reap the benefit of your hard work is to apply what you have learned to practical examples.

For your toolkit

T6.1 Trust is not ensured by believing it ought to be, or wishing that it is, practised.

T6.2 Risk and trust are inseparable, and their inextricable connection must inform your behaviour.

T6.3 Affirmations of trustworthiness are unreliable and must be tested against their behaviour because co-operating with a defector leads to your exploitation.

T6.4 Apply the rule: ascribe to others the motives that are safest for your self-preservation.

T6.5 If someone defects, assume that they intend to exploit you and not to protect themselves.

T6.6 In a one-move game, you may defect not because you want to but because you must – it is the best option for you, given all the possibilities open to the other party.

T6.7 In repetitive games, you may follow a tit-for-tat strategy. Initiate co-operation and then respond to the other party's play. If they defect, you defect (and quit the game). If they co-operate (even after defection) in a repetitive game, you respond instantly by co-operating.

Chapter 7
Jousting with Slobovic

➡ RED NORMS

Red 'taking' behaviour, in my experience, is the behavioural norm of the majority of business negotiators. It is induced by short-term desires to grab the quick buck. A passion for the immediate gain swamps consideration of future gains.

Examples include selling behaviours motivated by quota targets and not the needs of the customers. When computer sellers saw their job as the 'shifting of boxes' if they were under quota, and holding sales back if they were over quota, they transformed computer procurement into a choice between mere commodities, which undermined the big brands.

A new managing director, who took over a profitable manufacturing plant, noticed the large number of CAD and CAM systems that were lying around in various states of disassembly and disuse and, on enquiring, was horrified to discover that many of them had arrived without arrangements for training in their use. That these machines would aid production was not in question, but the computer sellers had 'shifted boxes' and had done nothing to integrate them into the company's manufacturing system or train the staff to use them. The MD immediately suspended all purchases from the computer company and announced that not another computer would be purchased until those they had bought contributed to output. It took the computer company – at its own expense – ten months to train staff to use the machines, and they never recovered their sales relationship with the company.

Red behaviour that undermines relationships means the parties do less well than they could for themselves and for their clients. Those who realise this may still have difficulty changing the negotiating games they play. Disillusioned red behaviourists, plus perplexed blue victims – of which there is a steady stream temporarily in recoil from extreme red behaviours – often fail to benefit from seeing advantages of another approach. They try this or that remedy to red play and, when all else fails, revert to red behaviour. Unlike addicts, who 'only' have to stop feeding their addiction, the disillusioned red player has to do something else besides 'only' stopping playing red. Meanwhile, if such players continue negotiating and find nothing to replace red play, sadly the result is predictable: they revert.

Activity 7.1

Have you suffered from red behaviour recently? Has this led to your wanting to do something about it?
   Review what you have done about it and assess its effectiveness.

How can you develop skills to deal with red behaviour, particularly of the most personally upsetting kind – for instance when a red player bullies, insults, and taunts you? If this has not yet happened to you in a negotiation, in time it will, unfortunately, because there is a type of negotiator who uses red ploys to get his or her way and you will meet such a player eventually.

In some business sectors, such as where large numbers of busy people interact under stressful time schedules, red behaviour is more common than others, even endemic. Construction sites, editorial floors in the media, entertainment and venue management, kitchens in busy restaurants, and accident-and-emergency hospital units are some examples.

➡ THE SLOBOVIC CASE

Take the case of a Financial Director, Gunter Slobovic, whose formidable reputation as a hard-nosed negotiator precedes him wherever he goes. He does not easily agree to anything if it costs money, and he does not indulge in social pleasantries, except to finesse concessions.

Gunter is unfriendly. He is always in a hurry to finish a meeting. He gives the impression that whatever time he spends with you, the people waiting for him suffer a supreme sacrifice if he stops long enough to say 'hello'. So he doesn't say much, except 'goodbye', or an almost inaudible grunt.

Slobovic's manner intimidates most negotiators. The smart ones usually drop their company's paperwork on his secretary's desk and get out as fast as they can. Those (few) brave enough to stay and conduct their business suffer all manner of indignities, including waiting well beyond their appointed interview time and, if finally they get to see him, enduring constant interruptions. Gunter also makes it obvious that he is not listening, sneers at their company or its services, and regularly threatens dire consequences if they fail to 'sharpen their pencils'. In short, Gunter Slobovic is a difficult person with whom to deal. Only his firm's growth and strong profitability save it from being deserted by suppliers because it is more trouble than it's worth. Over the years, several firms have ceased trading with Gunter because their representatives could not endure the stress of dealing with him.

During negotiations his behaviour includes bad and abusive language, highly prejudiced expressions about 'foreigners' and 'young whippersnappers', and outright rudeness when defending his outrageous statements. Also he theatrically switches off his hearing aid when he doesn't want to listen to complaints about his late payments, announcements of price increases, or refusals of the concessions he rudely demands.

Have you got the picture?

When did you last experience anybody remotely like Gunter? Even, are you a 'Gunter' type? – I'm just asking, as you don't frighten me!

Select from the persons in your life who are similar to Gunter (they need not be perfectly like him, as he is a uniquely difficult person). Hold your image of the person you identify as like Gunter. For a moment just get their face into your mind's eye and run through your internal video to refresh your memory. You are going to revisit him or her throughout this chapter.

Admittedly, Gunter is a particularly nightmarish person with whom to deal, and while the world is not full of Gunters, there are still plenty of them around. If you include all the people who – even momentarily – behave like petty versions of Gunter, extreme red behaviour is an unpleasant feature of the rich tapestry of business behaviour.

Most probably, you will do what people usually do when they clash with people like Gunter. You will get angry, shout back, express your feelings and let them know what you think of them. You also tell your confidants of your lousy day, how you felt and how you reacted, and for your sake you hope your boss is not too censorious if your conduct hurts the business.

Activity 7.3

How do you respond to Slobovic-like behaviour? Is your response similar to the one I have described above? For example, do you let him or her know what you think of their rude behaviour and, if so, how and when?

Thousands of negotiators have described to me the strategies they use to deal with 'difficult' negotiators. Sometimes, to aid recall, I recount the story of Gunter Slobovic.

➡ MATCH OR CONTRAST?

Broadly, these negotiators describe strategies that *match* and those that *contrast* with a difficult person's behaviour. Occasionally, somebody describes a complex strategy to match and contrast at the same time! Rarely does anybody offer anything besides matching and contrasting as counter-behaviours and therefore I conclude, given the numbers questioned, that the majority of practitioners claim to respond to difficult behaviour with dead-end strategies.

Note, parenthetically, that I have never met a negotiator yet who admits being 'difficult' in any sense remotely like Gunter. Every-body with a modicum of business experience claims to have dealt with a Gunter at one time or another, and yet none of them ever behaves like him! I mention this extraordinary phenomenon for students of selective memory syndrome!

Before we consider tools for dealing with difficult negotiators, we must first dispose of the two dead-end strategies of matching and contrasting, if only because of their prevalence among practi-tioners. 'Matching' and 'contrasting' purposely support the objec-tives of changing the difficult person's behaviour as a prelude to negotiating a better outcome.

On a tactical level, what is matching behaviour? Briefly, you play red against red, with the private proviso that you are only pretending to be red. If Gunter shouts, you shout; if he interrupts, you interrupt; if he swears at you, you swear back; if he threatens, you counter-threaten; if he intimidates, so do you; and so on through the long list of Gunter's red behaviours. Asked what this behaviour is supposed to achieve, practitioners offer versions of: 'It shows Gunter that I too can be difficult and that I am not afraid of "mixing it" with him.' In short, 'He can't intimidate me.'

What then is 'contrasting' behaviour? Briefly, you play blue against red, with the private proviso that you are only pretending to be blue. Thus, if Gunter shouts, you speak quietly; if he speaks quickly, you slow down; if he interrupts, you give way; if he swears, you don't; if he threatens, you ignore his threats; and so on through his repertoire of behavioural atrocities. People answer the question: 'What is contrasting supposed to achieve?' with some version of: 'Gunter can be as difficult as he likes, but against my contrasting responses his crude demeanour is somewhat ridiculous compared to my polite manners.' In short, 'His intimidation can't work on me.'

In my workshops, lively scenes follow as we debate the pro's and con's of these strategies. Strangely, the contrasters, while enthusi-astically elucidating on the merits of their strategy, often become as heated as the matchers, which suggests that contrasting is fragile as a pretensive behaviour.

Flaws in matching and contrasting

Both strategies suffer from flaws – some of a practical nature (they are difficult to maintain in practice) and others theoretical (they require differences in the response to the same behavioural stimuli).

Gunter is supposed to react to your matching or contrasting tactics by toning down his red behaviour. But why should he do that? If you match his red behaviour, you are not toning down your behaviour, are you? You are doing the opposite to what you expect him to do in reaction to your red matching behaviour. He is more than likely to follow your example and react to your red behaviour with more of the same. And if you contrast his red behaviour with what he perceives as blue submissive behaviour, he is likely to continue his red behaviour because your apparently submissive reaction confirms the efficacy of him playing red! Both strategies, therefore, rely on manipulation to change his behaviour.

Practitioners should always check the 'hit rate' for a recommended behaviour (i.e. the percentage of times that it led to a favourable outcome) and, in this situation, Gunter's hit rate from using red behaviour exceeds by a wide margin the hit rate from your counter-manipulation.

Activity 7.4

Think back to the last time that your choice between a matching or contrasting strategy worked, i.e. it successfully led to the conclusion you sought from the difficult person. Recall the negotiable issues, the behaviours of the other party, and how your strategy affected the outcome.

Also, recall the times when what you attempted did not work. Be honest, and estimate the 'hit rate'. If my assumptions are wrong, write and tell me why.

One of the problems of seeking advice on behaviour is that everybody has opinions but few test them in practice. Add in the proclivity for advisors to kowtow to the legendary Miss Goody Two Shoes and you have good reasons to be wary. For one thing, you ain't negotiating with Miss Goody Two Shoes, and, for another, neither is Gunter Slobovic.

➡ MIND YOUR OWN BUSINESS

What then should you do if matching and contrasting are not viable as strategies? The answer, at first glance, seems wildly counter-intuitive. It grows from an improbable and, for most people, uncomfortable assertion, namely, that the behaviour of other people is not really any of your business.

'What do you mean that a Gunter's behaviour is none of my business? Of course it is! He makes it my business by sticking himself and his **** behaviour in my **** face.' Wow! I got you going over this one. And if you feel that strongly over somebody else's behaviour, I can see why difficult people cause you so much grief! Take a break, have a cup of tea or something, and resume reading when calmer.

Minding your own business is not as shocking as it sounds. Neither does it mean you behave like a psychopath, unconcerned and unaffected by normal emotions. It simply asserts that you are responsible for your behaviour and not that of other people. Their behaviour is not a negotiating issue. By making their behaviour an issue, by which I mean making how they behave a precondition for how you behave, you commit a serious behavioural mistake. True, it is a common mistake, shown by the number of respondents who act as if other people's behaviour is an issue, but it is still an avoidable mistake.

Activity 7.5

Why do you think Gunter has a record of behaving the way he does, and why does he keep his job when his red behaviour is no secret?

If you answer to Activity 7.5 that Gunter's behaviour is beyond explanation, or that it is due to his personality, or that he 'blackmails' his Chief Executive, or that you just don't know, then you haven't tried very hard. You only hit the bull's eye if you answer that he behaves the way he does because it gets him what he wants. People bully and intimidate in negotiation not because of their psychological propensities (though I can't discount that as a possibility) but because they believe their behaviour works.

Survey your own or somebody else's habit of behaving in some definite way because they think it works for them.

Do children you know throw tantrums to get their parents' attention? Do any adults you know create 'scenes' to get their way? Who do you know whose behaviour can be said to be manipulative in certain circumstances?

If shouting at sellers induces concessions, the reward of easy concessions induces shouting; if sulking induces sympathy, whenever you want sympathy you sulk. Behaviourists have long researched the connection between stimulus and reward (though some of them appear to me to go over the top and make more of the connection than is prudent), but you too can recognise the connection between being difficult in behaviour and its expected reward. You strongly reinforce the beliefs of the difficult person when you allow their behaviour to succeed, because what works is replicable. You even weakly reinforce their beliefs when you make an issue of their behaviour. You, their 'opponent', they reason, only criticise their behaviour because you want to weaken them in the negotiations.

And remember, anybody can pretend to be extreme red to achieve their ends, in the same way that you can pretend to be red when you try a matching strategy. You do not monopolise deception. Red play is Slobovic's manipulative strategy to intimidate you into accepting his version of the negotiated outcome. He too plays these games, and if you rise to his bait, he wins. No wonder he keeps his job, and the esteem of his Chief Executive.

It is not the point that the reasoning of difficult negotiators includes fantasies and denials that there is anything wrong with their bullying behaviour. I do not wish to argue with them about their illusions and self deception, for I am in the negotiating rather than the counselling business. Confronting them over their behaviour with the intention of changing it is unlikely to succeed.

Taking them aside to let them know how uncomfortable you are
with their behaviour is suggested by some 'experts' in interpersonal counselling, but I doubt whether they have researched the
effectiveness of that tactic. By confronting them with your
opinions of their behaviour, you add a mountainous agenda of
interpersonal criticism and counter-criticism to the, perhaps,
substantive agenda you must negotiate with them. In my experience, from the moment you make their behaviour part of your
business, you complicate the negotiations.

➡ A SELF-DENYING ORDINANCE

You can nevertheless legitimately undermine the strategy of
intimidatory behaviour, namely by breaking the connection
between their bullying behaviour and the negotiated outcomes
they seek. Unconsciously submitting to their bullying connects
their behaviour to the outcome; consciously making their behaviour into an issue has the same effect. But suppose, instead, you
adopt the counter-intuitive and self-denying ordinance that however their red behaviour expresses itself, you will not allow it to
affect the outcome. They may behave how they like because you
do not care – it's none of your business – and what doesn't affect
your behaviour does not, and cannot, affect the negotiated
outcome.

Activity 7.7

Practise repeating the mantra, until you adhere to it unconsciously,
that 'the behaviour of other negotiators is none of my business'.

What at first is counter-intuitive only seems so when you
succumb to the habits of a lifetime and react to their behaviour.
You learnt those reactive habits at infant school. Push came to
shove and you pushed back, as you would observe (now that you
cannot remember your own school-dinner queues) if you have
ever tried to keep little children in a straight line. Where you
couldn't push back – the pusher was stronger, wilder and uncon-
trollable – you complained to your friends, sometimes even to

adults (earning derogatory epithets such as 'snitch', or 'grass'). You began your lifetime habit of trying to enforce behavioural rules that suited you, while as futiley expecting others to obey them. You made other people's behaviour your business.

Instead, get into the same mental state during your negotiations that protects the other negotiating party from your behaviour, namely a cultivation of a total lack of concern about their behaviour. Practise this when you attend meetings.

Activity 7.8

In any meeting there are items that do not interest you, and in some meetings nothing may interest you. When either of these happens, consciously disengage from the fray, particularly when all around you are losing their heads. Observe your colleagues' behaviour divorced from its content, and observe how they behave when the content is important to them. The more emotional they get, the better. Look dispassionately at how they behave, and what happens when they lock horns with those who oppose them.

If you are aware of so-called hidden agendas (such as rivalries, jealousies, the collateral fall-out from the termination of *affaires de coeur*, petty acts of revenge for earlier atrocities, and such like), this is all the better for your understanding, because intimate awareness of these subtexts enriches the value of your observations.

If tempted to join in and separate the petty squabblers, or side with one person against another, or when somebody's conduct irritates you, resist the temptation. The more dispassionate you remain from watching others make behavioural mistakes, the quicker you will improve your behaviour. You will soon be able to transfer your newly created dispassionate habits from the contests that don't affect you into the contests that do.

Apply the technique of cultivating dispassionate observation to meetings that address your interests, and practise extending your dispassionate observations to those who obstruct, frustrate and deny you what you want. In time, applying the mantra that 'their behaviour is none of my business' will become so natural that you wonder how you believed its opposite.

➡ BEHAVIOUR AND THE OUTCOME

I introduce now the second part of the counter-strategy to deal with the behaviour of difficult people.

Once you have managed to convince yourself that their behaviour is none of your business, then their behaviour will not affect the outcome. From then on you're home and dry. There is, however, one question that regularly pops up and that is: 'When should I, if ever, make it explicit to a difficult negotiator that their behaviour will not affect the outcome?'

The circumstances where it might be appropriate to do so vary, just as there are many circumstances where doing so is *not* advisable, especially when your explicit statement is taken as a challenge and provokes a contest of wills. Declaring you will 'pay any price, bear any burden' is good rhetoric when it is general, but making it too specific and too personal is not a good idea.

There *are* some occasions when it is necessary to establish explicitly that there will be no connection between their behaviour and the outcome. I refer here to sanction disputes, such as strikes, hostage stand-offs, and predatory business behaviours, but I assume you have some way to go before you handle these complex and serious negotiating crises. When you make it explicit to all involved, or privately for personal clarification, the common denominator must always be that the disconnection between their behaviour and the outcome is irrevocable, not negotiable nor subject to appeal. Unless you have total control of the resources and the unchallenged will to carry through this strategy, it is best to consider the circumstances carefully. A bluff called had better not be a bluff: only if the perpetrators of difficult behaviour reassess their ability to intimidate you will they desist from red behaviour.

I shall mention the last element in the strategy for dealing with difficult negotiators rather than elaborate on it at this juncture. If behaviour is not going to affect the outcome, what will? You, and the difficult negotiator, have a right to know my preliminary answer. The only way that the two parties can affect the outcome is by the negotiated exchange of proposals that give you some of what you want and give them some of what they want – in short, a traded exchange.

This is the core principle of negotiation. It is neither red nor blue but purple, and in the following chapters I supply the necessary behavioural tools for you to implement it in full.

For your toolkit

T7.1 Do not try to 'match' or 'contrast' a red player's behaviour.

T7.2 How Miss Goody Two Shoes might behave is no guide to how negotiators behave.

T7.3 Repeat the mantra regularly until it is automatic: 'Somebody else's behaviour is none of my business.' Disconnect their behaviour from influencing the outcome.

T7.4 The outcome of negotiations should be influenced only by the principle of trading.

Chapter 8
Sitting next to Nellie

➡ WHAT NELLIE DOES

I assume that you are an adult working in a culture and in a language with which you are familiar and that your colleagues expect you to take (perhaps new) responsibility for your department's complex negotiations.

True, in many jobs there is no induction period, no gradual easing into your role, and no period during which you may make mistakes. Work, which is a large part of modern life, is not always designed for our convenience. A mortgage is an antidote to interviewee humility, such as when a job famine spurs you to affirm that you already can handle what you have never handled before. Revealing the truth, you fear, disqualifies you from serious consideration.

Let us assume, therefore, that you are working yourself into a new job and that the job entails negotiation. Your familiarity with red and blue behaviours is more than most people have in your position. The simplest way to learn is through the venerable practice of 'sitting next to Nellie', a lovely person but not one of nature's best trainers. Sitting next to Nellie, who ignores you, and watching what she does, you imitate her behaviour at your next negotiation. You pick up her habits, good and bad. Sitting next to Nellie in many jobs is the full extent of an organisation's training policy. Some organisations don't even *have* a policy, and a few have never even employed a Nellie to put newcomers through their paces.

For a start, Nellie (and her cousin, Nigel) reek of attitudinal prejudices about their work (of their personal lives I have no information). Nellie's and Nigel's long experience comes from negotiating within their discretionary levels. They practise Jerry Rubin's admonition (when he was ultra-radical) in the title of his book *Do it!* So they do, mostly without thought.

Do not, however, arrogantly underestimate Nellie. She may not have an MBA but she is street-smart and memorises a vast amount of data, most of which she has difficulty explaining to beginners like you. Patience is not one of Nellie's virtues. Despite appearances, you can learn from watching Nellie or Nigel. They don't give it to you on a plate, nor do they soft-soap you. You must work to benefit from their experience and must discriminate between what they are good at and what they aren't (and never ever comment to them on the difference).

Activity 8.1

Who are the Nellies and Nigels in your organisation, who you could observe negotiating? Seek them out and find a way to persuade them to take you along. Promise not to – and do not – interfere.

➡ NELLIE NEGOTIATING

Suppose Nellie is to meet with Gordon, the sales representative of a luxury liquid-soap company that aspires to become your company's supplier of all your soap-dispensing toiletry needs. As this would be a sizeable order, Gordon will not expect a quick sale from one visit; one–hit big sales like that are rare at this level.

Suppose, also, that Nellie intends to invite Gordon to supply a couple of the offices contracted to your facilities company, to see how her customers react and – just as importantly – to see if Gordon's company delivers on his promises. Buyers, like courted partners after consummation, find that the person who paid court to them is long on promises and short on delivery (hence neither 'cynical buyers' nor 'disappointed lovers' is an oxymoron).

Gordon, of course, considers Nellie's news of the trial of his soap products a sales breakthrough. He discusses the details, such as the number of toilets per floor, number of wash-stands per toilet, the numbers employed per floor, plus whether there are hordes of visitors per day and similar things.

Eventually, a short silence intrudes, which portends a critical shift in every negotiation.

Activity 8.2

Gordon knows what is coming next and so does Nellie. Do you?

Yes, they turn to the vexed question of price. Whoever says pricing is a science confuses the scientific study of how negotiators arrive at prices with the unscientific process by which they arrive at them by negotiation. Observation of, and intimacy with, pricing processes in several business sectors suggests to me that so-called 'scientific' pricing is a fable agreed upon by people susceptible to pretentious humbug.

Communism collapsed not just because of its hideous tyranny, but because Soviet planners, in flat contradiction to the evidence, claimed to know in advance the price of everything. While, thanks to the KGB and the Gulag, they published prices for everything, the prices they published did not correspond to economic reality. Capitalists do not know in advance the price at which anything sells because markets decide the validity of a seller's assumptions (and a buyer's intentions) about price. For example, while I was writing this chapter, an entrepreneur who owns an exotic furniture business complained in a press interview about people being 'shocked' by her 'high prices', but, she bleated, they 'don't realise what it costs to make my designs'. What it costs her to manufacture her furniture explains nothing about people's antipathy to her prices! Capitalists, like forsaken lovers, are sometimes the last to know the truth.

Opening prices

Gordon at this moment is in the predicament of all negotiators: 'At what price shall I open?' Nellie faces the same predicament: 'What price shall I offer?'

As an observer, at what price do you think Gordon should open?
While you are at it, what should Nellie's price be?

An unfair question? Certainly! The only reassuring news is that you are not alone in wildy guessing the answer because neither Gordon nor Nellie knows of a formula that will give them their answer.

Gordon thinks he knows above what price he must charge to make a profit; Nellie thinks she knows below what price it is worthwhile for her to pass the deal for approval. But neither of them knows what the other thinks they know. Moreover, Gordon prefers the price to be higher than the least he can accept and Nellie prefers the price to be lower than the most she can pay. And now it gets interesting, because somebody has to quote a price if they are to make progress.

No matter how low a price buyers pay, they still prefer it to be lower, and no matter how high a price sellers accept, they still prefer it to be higher. Any negotiator denying this applies to them is being, er, disingenuous. All kinds of factors intrude on Gordon's or Nellie's perceptions of what is possible.

Gordon may be willing to sell his product at full cost plus 10%, or at the break-even price, or at marginal cost, or even below marginal cost to secure a foothold. He might, therefore, loss-lead his sale to Nellie and rely on his colleagues to make profitable sales elsewhere. (Of course, if all his colleagues loss-lead too, his company will not remain in business.) Nellie does not know what Gordon is up to when he quotes a price. She cannot see inside his mind. She might be of a red disposition and assume that Gordon heavily pads his opening price. She might be a true blue and believe that Gordon's price has the provenance of a Stradivarius. How she perceives the art of buying and selling drives her behaviour in the haggle that follows.

While imagining yourself sitting next to Nellie and across from Gordon in our example, practise deriving from their behaviours the colours of their attitudes and, from expressions of their attitudes, the colours of their behaviours.

With practice, you acquire the ability to 'read' speedily and accurately the behavioural intentions of negotiators.

First offers

Experience teaches negotiators not to accept the first offer, though red and blue negotiators draw different conclusions from their experience.

Red buyers (the majority), from prejudice borne of suspicion plus tinges of paranoia, assume that sellers pad their prices to fool guillible buyers. Hence, 'smart' buyers must always challenge first offers, no matter how good they appear. Extreme reds even discount squeals of despair as sellers slash their opening prices, believing it is mere play-acting on the 'cheating' seller's part. Blue buyers (a rare breed indeed), from conviction and a little gullibility, assume that what a seller affirms to be true is mainly true. Their responsibility, as a negotiating partner, however, extends to not behaving in such a manner as to provoke regrets on the seller's part.

Sometimes, low opening prices pleasantly surprise buyers when compared with their expectations. The blue buyer does not jump in and grab the deal enthusiastically ('yes, yes, a thousand times yes') because the seller would realise that they could have opened higher. So they too challenge the opening offer, not from red suspicion so much as from their blue concerns for the relationship.

Watching Nellie challenge Gordon's prices, which in your view appear eminently reasonable, even mouth-wateringly seductive, you could become anxious in case Gordon walks out of the negotiations. But Nellie knows what she is doing and Gordon's training ensures he can repel assaults on his prices by red buyers.

What motivates Gordon to behave as he does when he sharply discounts his price is not accessible to either observers or participants. All you need presume is that Gordon is the best judge of his interests: if he sells too low he will go bust, and this reality is the constraint that keeps him solvent. Any price he chooses to quote is at least above his insolvency price. Likewise, the price Nellie appears willing to consider, no matter how high, Gordon assumes is below some ceiling at which it becomes unprofitable, even suicidal, for her to reach. If Nellie throws money at Gordon's products, he obliges by supplying her and lets the market judge the efficacy of her decision.

The haggle

The manoeuvring over price, just described, is the haggle. Gordon tries to find out what is the most that Nellie will pay, without disclosing the least he will accept, and Nellie tries the opposite. Price is a single quantum and negotiations on a single quantum are haggles. The behaviour of the haggler is a venerable tradition, common to traders in all cultures.

I have a copy of a haggle over a copper pot from an Indonesian rural market and it bears a remarkable resemblance to haggles over products in Scottish markets. You could switch the hagglers and, apart from the language problem, any one of them would be at home with either script. In fact, nobody could predict which haggle was Indonesian and which Scottish.

Activity 8.5

Recall when you were last in a haggle. What was it over?
At what price did you start? Where did the other party start? How often did you each move? What brought the haggle to a close?

In mass-market societies, haggling thrives in old-style market fairs, and survives in some countries, I suspect, as sponsored entertainment for tourists. It is also prevalent in the midst of some complex negotiations, when it suddenly appears, usually by neglect. For this reason, you need to become familiar with the imperatives of the haggle that derive from its simple structure.

Gordon measures the supply of his company's soap in litres. Not surprisingly, he sells soap at so much per litre. This is his price quantum of the haggle. And sellers like to present their prices in the smallest unit quantities they can because this produces apparently small prices. For example, a price of 1.16 pence per litre does not sound much, although it may be exactly the same as a price of, say, £80,000 for a year's supply.

Buyers, not surprisingly, prefer, or ought to prefer, to aggregate the price per litre into the largest sum they can to put the most psychological pressure on the seller. '£80,000 a year for soap!' exclaims the buyer. 'How can I justify that to the procurement panel? They'll think I am having a breakdown and need medical attention.' The buyer knows that the aggregate cost magnifies the focus of attention away from fractions of a penny, and therefore the larger the unit of price in contention, the larger the movement from the opening price that will be required to settle.

For instance, photocopier sales people – a breed within which some thoroughly dishonest people ply their nefarious tricks – quote comparative prices in pence per copy. By scaling the quantities upwards they show massive savings from signing long-term contracts. This way they combine disaggregation and aggregation to baffle gullible buyers with the proverbial excrement of male cattle.

For illustrative purposes, let us assume that Nellie's tactic of insisting on unit price aggregation wins over Gordon's efforts to disaggregate to a price per litre. Clearly, whichever units they choose must be the same, otherwise it is difficult to follow their moves in the haggle.

Take Gordon's opening position of £80,000 for a year's supply of soap. Nellie safely assumes that Gordon will settle for less than £80,000, though she has no way of knowing his lowest price. Gordon, however, does know that number, and exercising the omniscient powers of authorship, I know it too: it is £65,000. This is Gordon's bottom-line or 'exit' position as things stand before he haggles, and this gives him a haggling range of between his bottom-line £65,000 and his opening, or entry, position of £80,000.

Nellie chooses an opening position of £52,000. Gordon does not know Nellie's exit position but I do: it is £72,000, giving Nellie a haggling range of £52,000 to £72,000.

But be clear, neither Nellie nor Gordon knows all four entry and exit prices. They know three of the four only: each knows their negotiating range and the other's entry price, when it is revealed, but neither knows the other's exit price, which is not revealed.

The gap

Once they reveal their entry prices, the difference between them indicates the gap when the haggle starts. Gordon reveals £80,000 and Nellie reveals £52,000.

Activity 8.6

What then is the gap between Gordon and Nellie? (Hint: take £52,000 from £80,000.)

The question implied by the haggle is: can the two parties close the gap?

All behaviour from now on aims to close the gap through mutual movement, and preferably with the other party doing most of the moving. Nellie tries to convince Gordon that he has to move in larger steps – and more often than she does. In reverse, Gordon tries to induce Nellie to do the same. They haggle 'dance'.

Whether the haggle is successful depends on the relative positions of their exit points in the negotiating range – and, remember, neither knows the exit position of the other. Gordon does not know whether the least he would accept, if push came to shove, is less or more than the most that Nellie would pay. If it is more than Nellie would pay, then there is a gap in their exit positions and a deal is not possible unless one or both of them revises their exit position. (So, if the least that Gordon would accept is £75,000 instead of £65,000 as above, then agreement is impossible because the most that Nellie would pay is £72,000.)

In the example, Nellie would go as high as £72,000 and Gordon as low as £65,000, and because their exit positions overlap a deal is possible, in principle, at any price between £65,000 and £72,000.

Activity 8.7

To test your understanding of these points, imagine that you are Nellie with her exit position of £72,000 and in the haggle Gordon proposes that you accept a price of £72,000. What do you now know that you didn't know before – something that Gordon still does not know?

What should you do next?

Despite many attempts to circumvent the problem of negotia-tors not knowing each other's exit points, so far none has been successful. All fall down on their vulnerability to untraceable manipulation by the parties and, because it is possible to falsify the exit points that negotiators could reveal, affirmations of them are useless. The only test is empirical.

Closing the gap

If a negotiator accepts a proposal, then that proposal must be in her negotiating range between her hidden exit point and where she opened. If another negotiator moves to a position between her exit point and where she opened, then she knows – but the other party doesn't yet – that a deal is possible. It is important at this stage not to reveal to the other party by body language that a deal can be done; indeed, the admonition to challenge an offer remains valid, because if he moves he must be within his negotiating range. He might move again deeper into your negotiating range and even closer to your entry point.

To this point in the narrative I have discussed entry and exit points and negotiating ranges, gaps and overlaps, fairly abstractly, though the advice of always challenging an offer is neither general nor abstract. Like Nellie, 'do it'.

Nellie, as a red player, intends to move Gordon towards his lowest price, and once convinced that he is at, or close to, this price she decides whether to do business with him. Gordon intends to convince her that he is at his exit price, even though he may not yet be there, and uses verbal devices to try to convince her that he can move no more.

We can put content into these abstractions with advice about how to identify them in your negotiations.

➡ ENTRY PRICES

How do you choose an entry price? How long is a piece of string? Everything depends on context. Pricing, as suggested, is not a science. But neither is it a random lottery.

We negotiate because we do not know in advance the precise terms under which we might do business. Those terms become specified through negotiation. In a real sense, sellers and buyers suggest various terms and signify those that are not acceptable. Credible, defendable and realistic entry terms invite serious consideration, and, if they are unacceptable in their original form, the credibility etc. of the cases in support of them, with minor amendments, positively influences their acceptability.

Careless presentation of an entry position – picking numbers out of the air, for example – undermines negotiating credibility, sometimes irreversibly. Offering £2 million for a business with net tangible assets of £10 million and no debt could undermine your reputation for seriousness; reversing it and offering £10 million for a business with £2 million net tangible assets could provoke caution, if not over your seriousness, perhaps over your mental health.

'Aiming high' when selling reads 'tough', but it is also a fact that aiming high has a low hit rate. You certainly make bigger numbers when you aim high and get a deal, but if you make fewer deals it is not so hot as a policy, unless buyers are under serious pressure to make *any* deal.

In contrast, selling cheap to get deals has significantly higher hit rates than overambitious pricing, but slim profit margins from underpricing are hostages to fortune. For instance, to lower its gross price for marketing impact, BL priced the famous Austin 'Mini' below £400, and produced ludicrously low profits of only £7 per vehicle. They sold hundreds of thousands of Minis and still made huge losses because endemic strikes and disruption drained away all profits and added to costs.

Activity 8.8

Successful car dealers hire sales staff to sell their cars. Which sales teams are most successful:

(a) Those that consist only of sellers who always sell close to the top of the dealer's list prices?

(b) Those that consist of sellers, some of whom always sell close to the top of the dealer's list prices, and some of whom always sell closer to the bottom of the permissible range of the dealer's list prices?

(Hint: consider the hit rates of the two teams.)

➡ EXIT PRICES

If the chosen entry price must be credible etc., what of the exit price? It too must be credible. The exit price is the bottom line, the 'walk-away price', and the point where a negotiator decides that further negotiation is unrewarding.

The negotiation dance often provides reasons to revise the bottom line (sales persons almost always cross imposed bottom lines in hot pursuit of orders). The other side's presentations and the debate of what they propose can change previous assessments of what is possible, and flexibility is needed in order to respond to these new possibilities. For example, as you negotiate the purchase of an 'exclusive' licence with one bottom-line price, it could emerge that the sellers will accept a 'non-exclusive licence', which requires a new bottom line at another price.

Activity 8.9

When was the last time that you changed a predetermined bottom line as a result of the information you received during your enquiries or the negotiation? Have you noticed this happening while observing other people negotiating?

Entry and exit points set boundaries to your available negotiating range. Sometimes that range is very large and sometimes minutely small. In high finance, banks negotiate in a narrow range of a few 'basis points', each one a mere one-hundredth of a percentage point. In multi-billion pound defence contracts, for instance, the small change is in millions, or tens of millions, of pounds. In energy deals, the price is in decimal points of a penny per therm.

The overlap of the hagglers' respective exit points narrows the available settlement area to a smaller portion of the gap between their entry points (there is, of course, no settlement area if exit points do not overlap).

➡ **ZERO SUM**

The structure of the haggle imposes behavioural pressure on the hagglers. The game is zero sum because what Gordon gains by inducing Nellie to raise the price she pays, Nellie loses in paying a higher price.

The haggle is confined to a single dimension, usually but not always, that of price. In haggling each haggler moves towards the other to reach a settlement.

Pushed too hard to move and Nellie suffers from 'psychic pain'. She might sulk or angrily denounce Gordon's pressure on her to move. Likewise, Gordon feels psychic pain as he moves his price towards Nellie's. It is not, therefore, surprising that haggles can degenerate into bitterly fought verbal contests as each resists moving.

Activity 8.10

If two children must divide an apple pie between them and one demands 60% of the pie and the other demands 80%, clearly they both cannot be satisfied. If they each demand 50% can they be satisfied?

State the general rule applicable for other possible divisions of the pie in which both can be satisfied. (Hint: if one gets 60% how much does the other get? If one gets 30% how much does the other get?)

The sum of the gains made by Gordon in inducing higher prices from Nellie is exactly equal to Nellie's losses. Inevitably, in single-issue haggles, gains minus losses sum to zero (hence the term 'zero sum').

While the haggle is relatively harmless in the Sunday market or on your holiday, where it can be great fun, in other contexts it can be positively harmful and can dangerously excite entirely negative

– even murderous – responses. Indeed, haggles over intractable disputes, such as territory or incompatible ideologies and lifestyles, tragically can escalate to violence.

Managers who settle everything with their employees except the money face strikes when the cost of moving to a settlement is psychologically unacceptable to those seriously disappointed in their aspirations for higher wages. Naturally, employees compare what they are offered with what they first asked for, and not with how much more it is compared to their current wage. We seem to suffer these psychic 'losses' much more than we enjoy our real gains. Similarly, many careless commercial contract negotiations that settle everything except the money, leaving it isolated for solution, become quite bitter.

When the burden of a solution falls on a single prominent issue, it inhibits movement, particularly when negotiators feel they have overcompromised on the nonprice issues they mistakenly settled earlier in the negotiation. I will discuss remedies for this problem, and how to avoid it, when examining multi-issue negotiation in Chapter 12.

Haggling is a primitive form of negotiating, and you should avoid sliding into a single-issue haggle when negotiating issues that are important to your interests.

In some contexts – tenders for major projects, for example – the buyer structures the bidding process in such a way as to enjoy the benefits of a zero-sum haggle in a one-way bargain. The buyer requires the bidder first to complete a technical negotiation, often involving heavy estimating and design costs, and then to complete a financial negotiation, almost certainly with the bid price as the main target. Separating the technical from the financial negotiations is to the advantage of buyers, which is why they use it; it puts maximum pressure on the seller, who is often under competitive pressure too.

That is why Nellie expects to drive a hard bargain with Gordon, who wants a foothold in Nellie's company.

Activity 8.11

What can Nellie do that will put pressure on Gordon to offer a lower price?

While Nellie evaluates the performance of Gordon's company and its prices, she reminds him regularly that her other suppliers remain in contention. She knows, as Gordon must, that his competitors will try to undercut whatever he painstakingly puts together if he leaves them opportunities to do so.

The haggle is fertile ground for red behaviour. Forcing movement onto a single dimension always invites red behaviourists to pursue results at the expense of relationships. Red buyers thrive in purchasing non-unique commodities. The less unique the products they procure, the more they exert leverage over competing sellers.

If they can issue tight specifications, competitive pressure from keen sellers drives down prices. Of course, the more complex the specifications, the less easy it is to compare bids, and in a drive to exert price pressure, buyers can overreach themselves by confusing sellers with the tightness of the specs. That is how the US Department of Defense ended up with a 29-page specification for oil cans, and ludicrously high unit prices to supply them, as contractors strove hard to meet the ludicrously complex specs.

Activity 8.12

How would you characterise the tendering process? Is it a red device to put pressure on sellers? Is it a device to protect buyers from exploitation? Do you think the tendering system saves money, or does it add to procurement costs? (Hint: who pays for the costs of all the lost tenders?)

Getting to sit next to Nellie, therefore, is educational because, by observing her at work, you practise identifying endemic red behaviours and she also teaches you something about the business you've gotten yourself into!

For your toolkit

T8.1 Always challenge first offers, no matter how beneficial they seem.

T8.2 Always expect challenges to your proposals, no matter how generous you make them (so don't make them too generous!).

T8.3 Convert prices into dis-aggregate and aggregate values for comparison, and then decide which to use.

T8.4 Establish your Entry and Exit positions for each negotiable issue.

T8.5 Select credible, defendable and realistic entry terms to invite serious consideration.

T8.6 Identify the opening gap between the Entry positions of the parties.

T8.7 When the other party opens or moves to your exit position, you know a deal is possible, so be careful that you do not give this information away by suddenly smiling, raising your eyebrows and leaning onto the table.

T8.8 Do not turn a negotiation of many issues into a red haggle over a single remaining issue.

Chapter 9
What do we want?

➡ RATIONAL PREPARATION

Few negotiations begin only after you meet the other party, though far too many people behave as if they need not to do anything until that meeting opens. Most negotiations begin when someone becomes aware that they have a problem and that they need to find and implement a solution.

Generically, you can summarise the sequence from awareness of a problem to finding a solution in the four minimum steps that are necessary for a rational decision by an individual. Briefly, these are:

1. awareness of a need
2. search for a means to satisfy the need
3. selection from the available options
4. satisfaction of the need

Activity 9.1

Apply the rational decision sequence to your awareness that you have a need to quench your thirst while you are watching your favourite tv programme. What decisions must you make to satisfy your need, bearing in mind that you have other needs competing for your attention?

Even applying the rational sequence to a thirst involves you in considerable mental work. Applying the rational sequence to complex negotiation problems requires prodigious amounts of mental work, not the least of which is reconciling the views of at least two individuals who may not share identical perceptions of each other's needs. We shall return to this later, but for now you should recognise the likely consequences of practices that neglect proper preparation to satisfy your needs.

Awareness begins long before the parties meet, and during the interval between the beginning of awareness and their initial meeting, the parties have the opportunity, and are wise to take it, to prepare themselves for what follows.

Key data

True, in some meetings you have no warning that there is to be a negotiation. Negotiations suddenly begin while you sit in a meeting, ostensibly perhaps called for another purpose. Or you answer the phone and find yourself speaking to another negotiator on a subject of her choice and at a time convenient to her but not necessarily to you.

Activity 9.2

Have you negotiated when you were totally unprepared? How did you feel? Embarrassed? Flustered? How do you think you performed?

In my experience, many negotiators act as if the surprise negotiation is the norm and the well announced negotiation is the exception. Put bluntly, they do not adequately prepare, and they fail to acquire the necessary details and data, or to select achievable objectives and the tactics necessary to achieve them. Being caught short without the files in front of you when you take a phone call is unfortunate; taking unread files into a negotiation (or even not bringing them!) is almost inexcusable, and at some managerial levels it is sheer incompetence worthy of the sack.

It happens, though. I attended a briefing meeting where the director of personnel, responsible for negotiating her company's wage bill, did not know what her company paid in wages each year. I also watched a sales director, who, when asked what proportion of a major client's business his company represented, had to ring his office to get the answer from his assistant. That was bad enough, but he compounded his error by repeating the phone call routine when asked what proportion this client represented of his company's business. His chief executive laconically suggested that he bring his assistant to the meeting, as she seemed better informed than he was.

In both examples, it was inexcusable not to know the key data for the negotiations. It may be that we would not expect the personnel director to know her company's business ratios, nor the sales director to know his company's pay bill, but they ought to know the key data of the functions they direct – if they wish to keep their jobs. Graham Day, on the morning when he became CEO of a loss making company sacked the financial director on the spot for being unable to tell him instantly that month's key financial ratios for the company. That sent a clear enough message about his expectations round the management.

Activity 9.3

What are the key data in your job? Could you answer immediately a direct question about them and give an accurate summary of the data? If not, why not?

With negotiation so ubiquitous, lack of preparedness is not so prominent and it is relatively easy to get away with incompetence. As most negotiations have few witnesses (with half of them on the other side) their colleagues seldom critically assess their poor preparedness. This induces laziness. And laziness in preparation makes for poor performance – and it shows in results.

Poor results obviously and ultimately act as a quality check on performance, but the perpetrators of the results they negotiate can give career-saving peformances when accounting for their poor results. Their listeners, not at the negotiations, cannot judge the veracity of their reports, and so poor performers get away with laziness and incompetence for long periods. Until, that is, some-one asks them questions about what they should know cold, and their inability to answer credibily exposes the reasons for their failings.

Graham Day's solution is not replicable everywhere. He had a low tolerance threshold and no time at all for anybody needing the luxury of long learning curves. If every unprepared negotiator was liable for dismissal, wholesale sackings would be the norm, but if you take seriously your responsibilities for your negotiations, the remedy for this avoidable problem – proper preparation – is firmly in your own hands.

Out-preparing the other negotiator is an advantage the other party gives to you by default, provided that you attend to the task they neglect. Your neglect, likewise, gives them the advantage. And lack of preparation shows. Bluster is a sign of someone trying to substitute gesture for preparation. Striking attitudes for effect is another. So are wild generalisations and making demands without consideration of how to move from extreme and indefensible stances towards solutions agreeable to the other party.

➡ WHAT IS THIS NEGOTIATION ABOUT?

The preparation sequence I recommend avoids 'analysis paralysis' and corresponds to what effective negotiators do when they mean business. Like a skilled artisan, first you learn what the tools can do and then you select those tools sufficient to complete the task. You do not need to use every tool available, any more than a mechanic uses every spanner in the box to loosen a single nut.

Ask the obvious question: what is this negotiation about? A price increase, a wage rise, contract terms, technical specifications, a relationship, licensing, loan finance from a bank, an acquisition, a merger or de-merger, a marketing campaign, an unpaid bill, a quality issue, a performance, a promotion, a pay-off, an agreed statement to the media, a retirement package, or a service agreement? These, and many others too numerous to list, are the daily fare of negotiators. Anything and everything is on a list that someone, somewhere, at some time, finds subject to negotiation. So answering the first question is not difficult. The next takes a little more effort.

➡ **WHAT ARE MY INTERESTS?**

What are my interests in this subject for negotiation? By 'my' I of course include any organisation you represent and serve, and for now let us assume for simplicity of focus that your interests and those of your organisation are identical. It complicates things when they are *not* identical, though by making a 'career decision', or a moral choice, you can resolve it.

First, what is an interest? Put simply, an interest is whatever motivates you to prefer your solution to the problem that is subject to negotiation. An interest therefore is the reason why you prefer this or that solution over those offered by the other party.

Employees, for instance, want higher wages because it is in their interests to improve their living standards (more choice, more security, the good things of life, prestige, etc.). Improving their living standards is an interest; the wage increase is the issue; and the amount by which they wish to raise their living standards is their position. A government wants peace with its neighbours because, while defence expenditures are expensive, the costs of fighting a war are many times greater. Peace is the interest; a non-aggression pact is the issue; and the terms of that pact are their positions. Or a third example: the security services do not prevent an assassination because this would expose their mole, who has deeply penetrated into the terrorist organisation. Preserving a long-term source of intelligence that will eventually defeat the terrorists is the interest; choosing which intelligence to act upon is the issue; not using the intelligence on this occasion is the position (but rather hard luck on the assassinated victim!).

Activity 9.4

How would you summarise the interests of your organisation? Pick a negotiable issue that is current in your relations with a supplier or a customer and identify the interests of your organisation in that issue.

Why is identifying one's interests worth the effort? Essentially, it is a reality check on the policies you pursue in the negotiation. For example, ignoring your interests you might pursue a pay claim into an economically ruinous strike that bankrupts the employer and leaves all the ex-employees worse off than they were without a pay rise. In other words, forget your interests and you may act self-destructively.

Naturally, there has to be a balance struck (I never said it was easy!). If your concern for your interests paralyses you from doing anything that might risk them, you would do nothing at all. For instance, a nation may be so keen not to risk a war that it makes it appear by its behaviour that there are no conditions that it will allow to jeopardise peace. An aggressive neighbouring state notices this and initiates actions that lead to invasion.

To ensure you understand the balance needed, it is best to specify your interests and judge how your negotiation behaviour and objectives will achieve them. Acting in ignorance of interests is foolhardy.

Issues and positions

By identifying your interests, you understand more clearly their relationship to the negotiable issues. Issues are the agenda of the negotiation. They are the joint decisions scheduled to be agreed with the other party. Their exact terms are the positions (quanta, forms of words, etc. relevant to each issue) that are also jointly decided by the parties.

Interests, issues and positions are interlinked. Some people make the mistake of thinking that interests are more important than issues, or that having positions is 'dangerous'. Such sloppy thinking is plain silly. Of course, to focus on one of the three (say, positions) and to neglect the other two would be inadvisable, as it would be inadvisable to focus on interests and to overlook positions. They are not in competition with each other; they are inseparable.

The negotiable issues deliver the interests; they do not deliver themselves. Peace between two countries without a negotiated relationship (usually by treaties, conventions and protocols arrived at through diplomacy) is an empty hope.

Activity 9.5

Think through why this last assertion is true in practice.
Why must peace be supported by detailed treaties, conventions and protocols? Why can't we just declare peace and leave our neighbours alone?

A treaty, unless it specifies its terms, is meaningless. For example, one position that it is necessary to specify in detail is the definition of each country's criteria for citizenship. This, and similar definitions, are derived from the positions negotiated by the parties. Without these definitions, policing at the frontier would be arbitrary and discriminatory and ultimately a cause of tension, thus compromising the interests of the parties in peace.

Positional bargaining is exhausting for those charged with undertaking it, but 'hard work ain't easy' and working long hours to settle definitional detail is not everybody's idea of a fruitful life. Attention to detail by would-be negotiators goes with the territory, and if you are averse to poring over detail, perhaps you should consider another career?

Compatible and competing interests

Interests may be compatible or competitive. An individual may have an interest in improving her living standards and in receiving training. These are compatible interests in some circumstances (she loses no pay during her training) and competitive interests in others (a temporary drop in her pay to undergo specialist training that leads later to a higher pay grade). She also has an interest in ensuring continuing employment, which might conflict with her interest in raising her pay.

Two individuals or organisations can have compatible and competitive interests. The classic examples are capital and labour, or buyers and sellers. Their compatible interests include continuing in a beneficial relationship; their competitive interests include zero sum differences about aspects of their relationship.

Another example of a compatible interest is that of safety in the workplace. Accidents interrupt work flows, which raise production costs; and they hospitalise the injured, which reduces their quality of life – perhaps permanently. Preventing accidents is therefore a common and compatible interest. Unfortunately not all employers and employees act in a manner that delivers their interests on safety. Some employers allow safe working practices to lapse through neglect, and some employees ignore safety procedures and even remove – yes, remove! – safety guards on dangerous machinery. While demolishing a university building found to contain asbestos, several employees offered to work overtime with only handkerchiefs for protection. I have also heard managers opine the cynical view that the difference between an 'unsafe' and a 'safe' working practice is (currently) about £1 an hour.

Which interests dominate at particular moments depends on what is at stake. There is no guarantee that each emphasises the same set of interests at the same time. Buyers may push their compatible interests with sellers who try to raise their prices, while the sellers may push for higher prices to serve their competitive interests of the need to make more profit.

Activity 9.6

Take your major external customer and identify your compatible and competitive interests.

Now think of the compatible and competitive interests you have with your largest internal customer (that is, the department or service that your department supplies with your output).

In some banking negotiations, the customer emphasises his transactional interest in pursuing opportunities with cheaper banks, while the banker emphasises her relationship as a more important interest over the longer term.

Activity 9.7

Under what circumstances do you think a bank customer and a bank switch their positions, with the customer in favour of relationship banking and the bank in favour of transactional banking? (Hint: think of the business cycle.)

Again, it is a question of balance.

Different issues, same interests

The other feature of interests that is of real and significant benefit in negotiation is the relationship between interests and the alternative ways of delivering them. An interest, in principle, is deliverable by more than one set of issues.

If you reach deadlock over one set of negotiable issues, with all the disagreeable consequences that that entails, and you consider instead the overall interests of the parties, you could address these interests through another set of negotiable issues.

Activity 9.8

Suppose two parties deeply disagree about their positions on whether to raise wages. What other ways can they improve living standards besides that of increasing wages?

The two parties could consider negotiable issues such as company pensions, longer holidays, shorter hours, training, and a host of others; and when the workforce becomes convinced that these other issues could deliver its interests in raising its living standards, that could be enough to break the deadlock.

In commerce, similar interest-based bargaining possibilities suggest themselves to those who start their preparation from their interests and not from whatever issue seems to be prominent. A German clothing manufacturer had an interest in financial viability and saw this as being achieved by receiving payment for clothes delivered to a British stores group 14 days after despatch. The British stores group also had an interest in financial viability and saw this as being achieved by paying 21 days after receiving the clothes at its warehouses. They had a similar interest – financial viability – and were trying to negotiate the issue of the date of payment, by anchoring themselves to incompatible positions (14 days after despatch or 21 days after receipt, to which 5–8 days were lost transporting the clothes from Germany to Britain). The deadlock threatened their profitable relationship.

Activity 9.9

Set out the negotiating relationship of the German and British businesses in zero-sum terms.

This example is a clear case where changing the means by which the two parties delivered their interests was the best way forward. Those familiar with banking practice may already have spotted that their resort to a well known and popular financial instrument, the Letter of Credit, would solve both parties' problem. Using a Letter of Credit, the German company received payment for clothes on despatch (less the bank's commission), and the British company paid its bank for the clothes 21 days after it received them (plus the bank's commission). The time at which the two businesses paid, and the bank's commissions, were negotiable issues that delivered their interests in financial viability.

Activity 9.10

Try re-examining a negotiable issue in your business by identifying your interests and then searching for different negotiable issues that could, in principle, deliver those interests. It is not necessary for this exercise for you to find a *better* way of delivering your interests; you only need to practise considering *different* ways.

The point is worth reiterating here, and Activity 9.10 demonstrates it, that proper evaluation of the linkage between interests, issues and positions, requires adequate time to complete the mental work. Preferably, you should do this calmly before you meet the other negotiator and not while under pressure during a meeting.

To be sure, if you have not prepared before you negotiate, then you will have to prepare, perhaps, in less-than-propitious circumstances. For this reason, sometimes, it is difficult to pull divisive negotiations back from the brink. This adds credence to the old saying that 'people who never have time to prepare properly before they meet always find time to do it properly later'.

➡ PRIORITISING INTERESTS

All interests are important but some are more important than others. Knowing the difference is helpful, and you are the only one that knows the difference in the importance of your interests. Some interests have overriding importance in one situation and less importance in others.

Your interest in personal survival overrides your interest in self-esteem on the deck of the *Titanic* if travelling alone, but you might put personal survival lower than the safety of others if travelling with your children. Similarly with the negotiable issues. Like interests, you may prioritise the negotiable issues while preparing. If you do not, then either you must treat all the negotiable issues as equally important, or prioritise them as you go along, and neither of these methods is satisfactory.

To prioritise the negotiable issues, sort them according to their weight in achieving your interests. In some circumstances, you weight the time when you are paid for your services (in advance, during, immediately on completion, or 30, 60, or 90 days later) over the amount you are paid (a high, medium, or low price), and vice versa in other circumstances.

Activity 9.11

In what circumstances lately did you consider *when* you were paid to be more important than *what* you were paid (or vice versa)?

A high-priority issue has greater impact in delivering an important interest than a low-priority issue, and it attracts a greater effort to secure what you want. The convertible currency a supplier receives in payment for its goods may be of less significance than the nominal price it agrees for the goods. In other cases, the reverse could apply because, although all convertible currencies are interchangeable, the supplier may prefer payment in its country's convertible currency rather than its customers' if the exchange risk outweighs a price advantage.

From such differences in priorities, negotiation is possible.

Activity 9.12

Think of a recent negotiation and segregate the negotiable issues into 'high', 'medium' and 'low' priorities (from your side's point of view).

Did your priorities for the negotiable issues differ markedly from the other side's? Can you recall how you became aware that you had different priorities?

Low priority gives high leverage

A caveat is appropriate here because sloppy thinking leads to sloppy behaviour. The act of prioritising interests and issues often sets unintended hounds off in pursuit of unhelpful behavioural hares.

It is all too easy to prioritise issues into 'high', 'medium' and 'low' classifications, according to their importance for achieving your interests, and then to conclude (falsely) that only the high priorities are worth anything. The notion behind what is important and what is less so carries the germs of potential error. It is easy to slip from the notion that a negotiable issue, of 'low' importance, is so unimportant that it does not matter what happens to it. Low-priority issues become unimportant, make-weight bargaining chips, and, in a final bout of silliness, give-aways. From being negotiable issues they become concedable issues. This is a serious error.

The purpose of prioritising is to determine each element's contributory weight to the achievement of interests and not to determine its tradability in the negotiation. What something is worth to you is not necessarily the same as what it is worth to someone else. If they consider it important to the achievement of their interests, while you do not regard it as important to yours, it does not invalidate its importance in the negotiation.

Negotiation is about exchanging movement on low-priority issues for movement on higher-priority issues. Your so-called low-priority issues, for the direct delivery of your interests, have indirect importance for your interests through the negotiated exchange. Which currency you pay in may have no great significance to you but may be of great significance to your supplier. Her country may be suffering, like Ogoland, from the self-inflicted ravages of exchange control, and payment in other than US dollars would seriously harm her profitability. Also, she may wish payment into an off-shore bank, which is not problematic for you. For acquiescing in her requests on your low-priority issues, you would seek to trade for reciprocal acquiescence by her on your higher-priority issues. And she will do likewise in reverse.

Hence, understanding the proper meaning of prioritisation of the negotiable issues avoids 'no problem-itis'. Negotiators who sprinkle their give-aways with exclamations that this or that is 'no problem' usually end up with a major problem: they have nothing left to give away and still have the important issues to settle.

➡ WHAT DO WE WANT?

When asked to summarise what preparation is about, I reply that it answers the question: what do we want?

Given the situation and the circumstances, you identify your interests and from them derive the most likely negotiable issues to deliver your interests. For each issue you decide upon your entry position (a quantum, a form of words, a 'yes' or 'no', etc.), which is the minimum you must do. For important issues you also form some idea of your exit points, if they are not readily obvious. These give you your negotiating ranges for all of the issues that form the agenda of the negotiation, although others might be added by the other negotiator or emerge during the negotiation if the original issues prove difficult to settle.

Some issues are more important in delivering your interests than others, which leads to the notion that priorities emerge from among the issues. Your priorities usually do not perfectly match the other party's because some that are important to you are of less importance to them. It is inevitable that you will think about the other party's possible priorities, but I emphasise that this should not feature too highly in your preparation time. Much of what you assume about them and their negotiating objectives will need revision once you meet them.

Your main preparatory task is for you to become familiar with the details of the dispute. Next, you complete some of the early manipulations of the data (most business negotiations require familiarity with spreadsheets, or at least a calculator). You should also be familiar with the paperwork, especially the details of the contractual terms.

Activity 9.13

If new to negotiations with a particular client, read all the letters and reports in the file. Summarise what you learn from what you read, in respect of recurring issues, and try to state your company's interests and priorities among the issues.

Command of the detail gives you confidence like no other preparatory act can. If the people you meet wrote the letters in the file and your predecessor's replies, they know much more than you and have an advantage if you haven't bothered to read what they wrote.

Lack of confidence shows in what you say and how you behave. Worse, you will know just how weak you feel. And if you know, the people on the other side of the table have a pretty good idea too, which is no recipe for success.

For your toolkit

T9.1 Practise applying the four rational decisions steps to satisfy a need: awareness of a need; search for options to satisfy the need; selection from the available options; and satisfaction of the need.

T9.2 Postpone telephone negotiations for which you are not ready – call the initiating party back, or arrange to meet them, when you are ready.

T9.3 Calculate and regularly confirm the key ratios or data within your responsibility.

T9.4 Formally state what the negotiation is about.

T9.5 For any negotiation, identify your and the other party's interests.

T9.6 Consider whether the negotiable issues deliver the defined interests. Decide which other sets of negotiable issues could deliver the interests.

T9.7 Consider which interests are compatible and which incompatible.

T9.8 Assess your priorities (high, medium, low) for the negotiable issues.

T9.9 What is your negotiating range (entry and exit positions) for each issue?

T9.10 Assess the bargaining leverage of your low-priority issues: how important might they be for the other negotiator?

Chapter 10
What do *they* want? Starting negotiations

➡ **FACE-TO-FACE INTERACTION**

The action now moves to the face-to-face phases of a negotiation. Unlike preparation, the action is in full view of the other side, who in their unscripted interactions react to what you say, to how you say it and to what they think you mean. You respond and interact likewise, making 'unscripted anarchy' an apt description of the process.

Hopefully, you remember the one great truth of all communication: the message you send to another person is not necessarily the one they receive. But communicate you must because negotiation without communication, if barely possible, is primitive and inefficient.

Activity 10.1

Imagine trying to negotiate with someone who does not speak your language nor you theirs, and neither of you speaks a third common language. How would you set about it?

How complex could the negotiations become if you confined all communication purely to sign language and gestures?

You know already that you drive all your negotiation behaviour by the mix of your red or blue attitudes. Learning how to negotiate as if the relationship between attitudes and behaviour is incidental or ephemeral for most purposes leaves you not much better off than you would be in the absence of training. Yet a great deal of negotiating training does just that.

This process is like a boxer planning what he will do in the fight and leaving out of the equation what his opponent will be doing while he carries out his plan. It is all right aiming to 'float like a butterfly and sting like a bee', but if the other guy fails to co-operate, you may end up floating down to the canvas. And some pre-planned, carefully thought-out tactical sequences that pass for a negotiation strategy often collapse at 'move two', because the other side doesn't do what your script says they must. The other negotiating party has not read your script; they came with their own. And if you train without preparation for the reality of what happens in negotiation, then you will do less well than you could.

There is an unlimited array of possibilities in negotiation, vastly more than even those available in a game of chess, with its strict rules of play (or 10^{120}, which is vastly greater than the 10^{70} particles said to be present in the visible universe). Negotiators interact *without* strict rules, and therefore there is an infinite variety of sequences of possible behaviours, rendering analysis of every possible negotiating sequence impossible to imagine.

It is useful to think of red and blue attitudes as products of natural selection. Their extensive replication in specific instances of negotiation is a product of natural selection combined with social evolution. The majority of negotiators who unconsciously contend with the difficulties of confronting red and blue behaviours also manage to make their deals. Therefore, you too can cope with difficult and unpredictable negotiating situations and, with training and practice, you will do better than merely cope with them.

Hence, we shall approach the opening phases of run-of-the-mill business negotiations with a realistic description of what happens and not what ought to happen, but always with the intention of you learning how consciously to achieve your objectives. You want to be more than a passive observer in a social process and want, instead, to be an active participant.

➡ AIMING FOR DOMINANCE

Through props

Red behaviour in the opening face-to-face phase attempts to secure dominance over the 'opponent'. Red players effect this by manner as well as by props (meaning the theatrical kind). Anthropologists trace the roles of the artefacts (and the artifices) of red players in establishing dominance to those of our predecessors, who used natural features, like high rocks and clearings, and man-made symbols, masks and totems, to ritualise tribal compliance. Do not, therefore, take modern artefacts for granted and forget their subtle roles.

Thus, when you enter prestigious offices looking for potential business, you enter a stage set to undermine your confidence and to weaken your resolve. The artefacts of prestige are not there for the benefit of the employees, who nevertheless appear to enjoy them. Vast auditoriums, fountains and works of art prominently displayed in the entrance to buildings make statements about the organisation being approached for business and, more subtly, about those that lack them.

Super swift and silent lifts, which are peopled by purposeful minions, and the inescapable procedures you must complete to pass the security systems all work on your perceptions and diminish your self-esteem with the inevitability of an algorithm. You are now a mere number in their control system, and if you want to do business with them, this is the only way they will do it.

Not all props are so visible or so obvious, nor do they always need heavy expenditure to set them in place. Largeness has its qualitative strengths, which is why corporations recite their turnovers, their employees and the number of countries in which they locate their activities, almost as a litany of their achievements.

Personnel in smaller companies also play the props game. They too flaunt their large desks, their corner offices, their exotic titles and their mobile phones. Mostly this is harmless as long as you don't let it get to you. Imitation is not just the sincerest form of flattery, it is also a pathetic way to impress. As your personal antidote to pomposity, keep in mind Charlie Chaplin's portrayal of the pompous dictator in his aircraft carrier-sized office.

Activity 10.2

Do a quick review of your clients and identify their props. Do any of them stand out as a particularly subtle form of intimidation?
  Now look for your own organisation's props!

Through behaviour

The dominance manners of the red player are less subtle than their props. 'In your face' behaviour is effective if you let it get to you. If they succeed, they trigger your lapse into a tolerable imitation of blue submissive behaviour.

Typically tiresome dominance behaviours include petty rituals of their cancelling meetings (sometimes without apology), their keeping you waiting for an appointment, their allowing interruptions, their shortening your meeting because of 'pressing' (i.e. more important) business, their taking phone calls – or making them! – and their referring you to minions to evaluate your proposals.

Activity 10.3

Have you recently been treated to dominance behaviour of the unsubtle kind? Conversely, have you – intentionally or unintentionally – behaved in a manner that could be taken to be domineering?

Stepping up a gear, red players initiate dominance ploys, such as insisting on 'preconditions' before the negotiations open. These preconditions take many forms – some openly provocative and some apparently innocuous, but of which there can be no doubt about their purpose.

Typically provocative preconditions include 'surrender and disarm before we talk peace', 'return to work before we discuss your grievances', and 'renounce your claims before we consider compensation'. They provoke resistance – and sometimes that is their intention – because acceding to them weakens the bargaining power, perhaps fatally, of the acceding party.

Also, if a party does not want to negotiate but for image reasons it does not want to admit this openly, it does so by imposing provocative preconditions. The other party has the choice of complying and negotiating under humiliating conditions, or defying the preconditions and not negotiating.

A proclivity for imposing preconditions reflects the power balance. For many years, IBM imposed 'vendor contracts', carefully pre-prepared by their legal departments to protect IBM's interests (which is why they were pre-prepared!) and if you wanted to acquire an IBM mainframe computer, no matter how big you were as a corporation, you had to sign IBM's contract. Similarly, if you wanted to use a Xerox photocopier, you could only do so if you signed a pre-prepared Xerox Corporation rental agreement; they would not sell you one of their machines at any price. The rental agreement, which tied users to buying toner, paper, maintenance and parts from Xerox alone, became a vertiable licence to make secure profits.

From a negotiating point of view, imposed preconditions reduce the negotiable issues to a handful over which the vendor exerts its full bargaining power against the buyer. Changing technologies and competition nevertheless eventually erode vendor power and give new options to pliant buyers. The PC undid IBM; the lapse of its patents undid the Xerox Corporation.

Buyers sometimes retaliate with their own imposed preconditions. The clearest example is in the tendering system. To sell to powerful corporations, you submit to their procurement procedures. You don't just walk up to the front desk at General Motors and expect an interview with the person who buys what you are selling. American corporations, no less than their Japanese counterparts, impose strict and time-consuming procedures on all vendors before they even consider whether to issue a purchase order.

Throughout what could be a long procedure, negotiations continue intermittently and under the shadow of the corporation's dominating influence, and it takes considerable mental discipline and fortitude to resist sliding into blue-behaviour submission.

Activity 10.4

How commonplace are preconditions in your line of business?

Does your organisation use them? Do your suppliers and customers?

Do enforced preconditions help or hinder your negotiations?

Try to recount the official rationale for these arrangements and still appreciate their unstated role as aids to negotiating dominance.

➡ ADVICE ON OPENING BEHAVIOUR

It is interesting to read advice to negotiators on how they should behave during the opening sessions. Variously, they advise you to establish rapport with the other party, to seek common ground, and to set a friendly tone. There is nothing wrong with this advice, of course, and you do yourself no favours by deliberately ignoring it. But it relies for its validity as an aid to successful negotiation on the other party playing the same, or at least a receptive, game.

Politeness, good manners, gestures of respect and willingness to listen are necessary etiquette for negotiators. Their expression certainly won't get you a worse deal, though they might not improve on the one you do get. They are not in themselves sufficient, however, to achieve your objectives.

Seen as manipulative tools, 'rapport building' may have a short half-life because people can see through the shallowness of someone who grins like a Cheshire cat while trying to sell them something. Choosing behaviours for negotiation is no less a trifle fanciful than choosing to behave blue to somebody else's red, irrespective of the continuation of their red play. Permanently co-operating in the face of permanent defection is the choice of gluttons for punishment.

I recommend that you abide by the etiquette of negotiation not because it is 'nicer' to be kind than to be cruel, but because polite behaviour is in tune with the tasks of the initial phases. If, as I believe it to be, the purpose of preparation is to answer the question: 'What do *I* want from this negotiation?', then the purpose of the opening phases of the face-to-face interaction is to answer the connected question: 'What do *they* want from this negotiation?'

Hence, advice to be cheery if they are grumpy etc. misses the point and echoes the fallacious choice between matching or contrasting, which I disposed of earlier.

Questioning and listening

To find out what they want, to explore their aspirations and to search for areas of flexibility creates the singular imperative of using the stance of questioning as your main behaviour. Finding out what they want requires you to ask questions and listen to their answers (and to question their answers). You need information that only they can give you authoritatively, and so ask for it.

Activity 10.5

At your next meeting – it does not have to be a negotiation – seek an opportunity to question someone closely on what they report or propose, so as to clarify the details. Ask supplementary questions too, and listen to the answers.

Observe their reactions to your questioning and note how these are positive if they think your motive for your questioning is benign, and negative if they think it is malign. Think whether you can cultivate your questioning style to provoke positive responses.

Platitudes abound on how you can sell what you want to them. Rapport-inducing mood music etc. as a prelude to telling them what you want, without answers to questions about what they want, is for shadow boxers. Until you know what they want, the negotiation cannot enter productively into the phases of proposing and bargaining. And nothing in negotiation, remember, really happens until you negotiate proposals and bargains.

Task yourself to be an active listener to the other negotiator. If she is playing a dominating red game and fires off salvoes of demands, don't be fazed by her pressure. Fire back questions and listen to her answers.

I coached a team once to do nothing but ask questions (detailed and supplementary) of a rival company attempting to take them over in a hostile so-called 'merger'. From initial concerns and trepidation, they turned the tables and grew in confidence as their relentless questioning unnerved the hostile bidders until even they became unsure whether they wanted the 'merger' to go ahead. It did, though, but they secured much better terms (and better redundancy packages) than those they had anticipated before the negotiations began.

Questioning is the most powerful tool in the negotiator's repertoire and heavily underrated in practice. If 45 minutes or more go by without a question, you can be sure that below-average negotiators are at work. They are talking too much and not listening enough. Each will be queuing to speak and when they cannot contain themselves, they will be interrupting, maybe even interrupting their interruptions!

Argumentative behaviour

When you focus only on your wants (and ignore the other party's), you will become aware of the increasing likelihood that you will not get them. Anxiety over pending disappointment causes frustration and erodes your prior intentions to behave like Miss Goody Two Shoes. This provokes a drift into attack-and-blame cycles and eventually into threat exchanges.

If lovers can fall out – and they do fall out on occasion, sometimes murderously – what chance do negotiators have when virtual strangers apparently stand in the way of their wants? 'Not much' is the answer. Argumentative behaviour is so much a part of negotiation that many recoil from its symptoms, without tackling its causes. Two people trying to achieve what they want from each other, in an informal and unscripted process, is difficult enough without adding to it the inevitable misunderstandings of them speaking past each other. So convinced are you of your case, be it the price you pay or the goods for what you pay, that you take the other party's resistance to your case as hostility to your interests. And people who threaten your interests are enemies, they are out to do you down and to refuse you your just deserts. What a cocktail of red passion that provokes!

Anticipating rejection by the other side provokes heavy expressions of why you must get what you want and hints of what dastardly consequences will follow your not getting it. And to demonstrate your determination, you demand more than you will accept. To demonstrate their firmness against your outrageous demands, the other side's behaviour mirrors yours, and they offer far less than you will accept. A clash of Titan-like rhetoric follows, with unpleasant moments, while mutual frustrations devoid of mutual listening work through the opening phases. You only appear to listen when either of you picks on phrases that 'prove' the perfidious intentions of the other.

Activity 10.6

Observe how people pick on words and phrases to criticise when they are in dispute over anything.

Are you aware that you do this? Probably not, but I bet you are aware when somebody does it to you.

Summarising

You cannot force the other side to listen actively to you, but you can force yourself to listen actively to them. And doing so pays dividends.

If you listen actively, you can give an accurate summary of what they said. By accurate, I mean a summary that they agree with, and not one you believe you heard.

Activity 10.7

Think how many times you have experienced an interchange in which someone says, 'You said so and so,' and you deny it, followed by the repetitive pantomime routine of 'Oh, yes you did' and 'Oh, no I didn't'.

Summaries need not be as frequent as questions but they should be more frequent than average negotiators apparently consider them to be necessary. They are certainly advisable when the other side tell you what they want and when they respond to your questions.

In summarising:

1. you check what they said
2. you inform yourself in a compact way

3. you give them an opportunity to correct your errors
4. you confirm to them that you listened

That, I believe, is an impressive dividend from making the effort to listen and then summarising what you heard.

Activity 10.8

Practise the art of summarising by summarising what you have just read about the four benefits of summarising (and without re-reading the last paragraph!).

Fortunately, the same act of listening that is necessary to summarise efficiently makes another and even more crucial contribution to your negotiation dance. To put this great benefit into its proper context, you must recall the strategic problem that all negotiators face.

Signalling

Every negotiation begins with at least two solutions for every negotiable issue – yours and the other party's. To agree, you require a single solution, probably different from either of the originally proffered solutions (unless one of you gives in to the other). Now, how do negotiators simultaneously assert the validity of their solution and move away from it without sliding down a slippery slope to surrender?

The answer is not at all obvious. Some negotiators, like rabbits fixated by headlights, defend their opening positions and, though knowing they must move and even wanting to move, because they don't know how to move, they don't. That is why I have called negotiation 'the management of movement'.

In practice, negotiators (in the main) manage to move using a behavioural tool they learn without having to attend a training course. They use the behaviour known as 'signalling'. They express the early statements about opening positions as absolutes:

We demand not a penny less than £1,000 per year salary increase.

There is absolutely no way we will pay that account.

It will be impossible to persuade the Board to entertain further delays to the issue of an Occupancy Certificate.

We insist on payment in full of our compensation claim.

The absolute words used ('not a penny less'; 'absolutely no way'; 'impossible' and 'payment in full') are typical of opening-round exchanges. If things stayed that way, no one would make progress in the negotiation. But by careful listening, you can manage not to miss the unannounced use of signals (and the main cause of missing the signals is through lapses from active listening). Also, responding with summaries means your listening behaviour attunes to subtle changes from absolute to relative statements:

We demand substantial salary increases.

Under current circumstances there is no way we will pay that account.

It will be extremely difficult to persuade the Board to entertain further delays to the issue of an Occupancy Certificate.

We insist on payment of some compensation.

Signals replace the absolutes: 'not a penny less' becomes an unspecified but by implication lesser 'substantial' amount; if 'current circumstances' change, then this removes the absolute 'no way'; what was 'impossible' is now only 'extremely difficult' and 'payment in full' reduces to 'some compensation'.

Activity 10.9

You use and respond to signals all the time, though you probably do not realise their significance. Think of recent disputes to which you were a party and try to recall the signals sent and received.
  If you cannot recollect any, how did people move their positions?

Signalling is very common and has evolved with language to modify statements. It is universal, though just as languages use different adjectival forms so social conventions may influence types of signals. But signal you must because, aside from auctions and pure price haggles, where movement is instantly reciprocated without explanation, in negotiation explanation is part of the influencing process that structures expectations. From changes in your expectations there comes an acceptance of the necessity for you to move.

A signal by itself does not denote much, but with an appropriate response – assuming that the addressee hears the signal – there is a possibility of movement. The signaller qualifies the previously absolute statement and listens for the response. If the response is wholly negative, by the signal being rebuffed, then the negotiation, unsurprisingly, stalls and perhaps sours, meaning that to repair the damage more time will be needed:

> No matter what you demand, there will be no salary increases this year.

> You will pay that account, or else.

> It doesn't matter how difficult it is to persuade your Board, we will not issue an Occupancy Certificate until you pay all arrears.

> Insist all you like, we are not paying any compensation.

On receiving these responses, the signaller retreats. Thought of possible movement stalls, and the struggle continues.

However, a signal acknowledged is the negotiator's bridge to movement. The signaller has not committed irrevocably to move (that would be the slippery slope!) and nor has the responder. Signals are hints of a possibility for movement and not the actual movement. A positive responder might ask:

> We are willing to consider some reasonable increases in salaries, so it depends upon what you mean by 'substantial'.

> In what way would the circumstances have to change for you to pay the account?

> How can we make it less difficult to persuade your Board?

> What compensation do you have in mind?

Responses do not initiate firm proposals, nor need you expect firm proposals immediately. They shift the battle from behind the absolute ramparts to a more flexible dialogue. Qualifications, exceptions, problems with the wording, and the linking of movement to cross-related issues all become possible once you break the fixations over opening positions.

Acknowledged signals are like safe-conduct passes from a deadlock to the more fruitful exchange of new proposals. The atmosphere changes from total intransigence to more fluid flexibility. Even if you cannot identify exactly what caused this change in the atmosphere, you will certainly be aware that it has happened. How you respond to the change will determine if the progress you have made will continue or if you will run into the sand again.

For your toolkit

T10.1 Identify the dominance props used by those you meet for negotiations.

T10.2 Identify the use of red ploys to assert dominance.

T10.3 Consider all preconditions the other party sets as dominance ploys.

T10.4 Demonstrate negotiator's etiquette in all dealings.

T10.5 Actively listen more than you talk in the negotiating exchanges.

T10.6 Question the other negotiator, actively listen to the answers – and question the answers.

T10.7 Summarise regularly, for understanding, for clarification, for self-assessment of what they want, and for reassuring them of your full attention.

T10.8 Signal, and listen for signals.

T10.9 Positively respond to signals by seeking and offering clarifications.

Chapter 11
Shaping the deal

➡ THE EIGHTY PER CENT RULE

Much can happen between the first signals that movement in the negotiations is possible and the first tentative proposals that incorporate possible movement. Observation suggests that the debate and discussion (and their associated arguments) about what each party wants takes up about 80 % of face-to-face negotiating. If debate proves inconclusive, or diverts into prolonged argumentative exchanges, the time span of the interaction extends absolutely and the debate takes up 100 % of the available time. Negotiators stuck in argument may never get to the exchange of proposals, or past their first exchanges, before they run out of time.

Red behaviour contributes to the middle phases of negotiation with no less intensity than is common in the opening phases. Only if a red player intimidates a blue player into submission does the negotiation conclude quickly with an agreement, albeit that it is one likely to be more favourable to the red player than the blue. Red play becomes dysfunctional, however, when a red player meets another red player and they slog it out until, wearily, one or both withdraws. Before learning how to deal with red play in the middle phases, you must identify its methods.

Confronting red play in the opening or middle phases in isolation from your proposing and bargaining behaviour is inadvisable, but for clarity of exposition we must suspend until later the exploration of what I have called 'purple' behaviour. Meanwhile, we shall examine what red and blue players get up to as they try to shape the deal before they exchange proposals for movement.

Red play involves ploys (sometimes erroneously called 'tactics', which gives tactics in negotiation an undeserved and disreputable aura). Ploys have a purpose and once you understand that purpose, identifying a behavioural act as a ploy neturalises its effect on you. Also, for every ploy there is a counter-ploy, and experienced negotiators who recognise red ploys become immune to those ploys that are relentlessly tried by red players.

Untrained negotiators learn the hard way. Many, of course, learn different things from their experiences. Some learn to replicate red play (and ploys) and come to believe it is necessary 'to do unto others before they do it unto you'. Others are already steeped in red attitudes long before they realise how good they are at applying them to negotiation.

➡ POWER PERCEPTIONS

Red players who perceive of negotiation as a competitive game between two opponents use ploys to influence the other negotiator's expectations of the outcome. They believe that everybody, like themselves, is influenced by their perceptions of who has the greater power in the negotiation. Perceptions are everything, and so if you manipulate someone's perceptions and they believe that you have the power, then for all practical purposes you do.

Activity 11.1

Who among your clients would you say had more power than you in your negotiations? Try to describe the sources of their power relative to you.

How real are these sources and how do they manifest themselves? Are they assumptions on your part, and merely cultivated 'facts' on theirs?

According to a red player's mental model, there is an inverse relationship between your perceptions of their power over you and your expectations of the outcome you are likely to achieve from them. Thus, if you perceive their power over you is greater than your power over them, you will have low expectations that the outcome will favour you. Conversely, if you perceive their power over you is less than your power over them, then you will have high expectations that the outcome will favour you.

Intuitively, this approximates to how people do in fact see the power balance. We talk of them being 'stronger' than we are, or having greater 'bargaining power', and how 'bargaining leverage' separates those with power from those without it. Ploys, then, work on your perceptions, which in turn lower your expectations. Putting it crudely, as a seller you would lower your price and as a buyer you would raise it.

Activity 11.2

If you joined the rear of a long queue waiting to view a house for sale, what are your chances of buying it below the asking price? Would you expect to pay well over the odds to buy that house?

Why do you think house sellers tell little white lies about the number of interested buyers ready to make them an offer, or the time the house has been on the market?

Red ploys are so common they long ago ceased to be infamous. Yet they continue in use despite their public unmasking and the familiarity of practitoners with them in everyday discourse.

➡ RED PLOYS

Take the clichéd tough-guy/soft-guy ploy. Only the very naïve, or aliens from another planet, fail to recognise somebody playing it. Of those who do recognise the ploy, a fair proportion report that they feel unable to counter it and cannot help but be a victim. This is an astonishing observation, for which I have no explanation.

The original good-cop/bad-cop ploy used two people, one acting as a tough cop and the other acting as a soft(er) one. The secret was not to let the target know you were acting; for him it was all too real. Several generations of filmgoers (and, more recently, tens of thousands of delinquents experiencing it at first hand) must have disseminated the ploy into common discourse, and by all accounts it should have declined in use.

Can you remember when you first came across the tough-guy/soft-guy ploy? When did you last hear it?

Maybe it has tended to disappear from police procedures, but it continues in negotiation, both as a double act and as a solo performance. I still meet negotiators who describe incidents they experience and seem surprised when I label their experiences as a version of the tough-guy/soft-guy ploy.

My earliest observation of the ploy was while watching a shop steward conduct a strike. They called him 'the Dentist', because his sole contribution at mass meetings of dockers was to shout: 'I've ony got one thing to say, lads: pull 'em out!' His timing was immaculate, and dockers at angry meetings, knowing what was coming, would finish off his single sentence speech by all shouting together: 'Pull 'em out!' At negotiations he sat at the end of the line of the officials, half facing them, and whenever his colleagues exhibited a modicum of sympathy for the company's position, he would glare at them, wide-eyed and intense. If his side signalled any movement, he growled and, occasionally, threw himself at any colleague who softened in tone or language.

His colleagues used him to justify their lack of movement and to encourage movement from gullible employers. They made their demands seem reasonable alongside the Dentist's absolute intransigence.

Can you recall examples of single persons playing a version of the tough-guy/soft-guy ploy?

When did *you* last use it ('my boss won't agree to that', or 'my partner told me to accept nothing less than £500')?

Solo efforts at the ploy also abound in commerce. They may be more genteel in their manners, but ploy players are every bit as deceptive.

The red player claims to be most sympathetic to your point of view but she has a procurement committee (or a budget committee, or a Board, or a boss, or a partner) who is positively 'Neanderthal' in the matter of reasonableness. Conveniently, these people are not present but she alleges that they make the final decisions. Hence, she can only work for your interests, and get a 'yes' for you, if you give her something she can present to the really 'tough bastards back at the ranch'. You react to the power play of tough-guy/soft-guy by lowering your expectations. You settle for less because you believe that there is no chance of more. If that is what you believe, then that is how you behave. You do not always realise you are behaving like a blue submissive because sometimes your reasons for behaving in these blue ways are totally believable.

Krunch, Killer, Nibble and Russian Front

There are many ploys, too numerous to enumerate here, available to red players. They all have in common an intention to shape the deal in their favour by shifting the centre of gravity of the settlement away from your initial expectations towards their notions of what is possible. The most famous ones – and they still work despite their fame – include, the Karass 'Krunch' (after Chester Karass, the doyen of negotiation seminar presenters), the 'Killer' and the 'Nibble'.

The Krunch simply tells you that 'you'll have to do better than that'. When timed to perfection, the seller is put on the spot. The buyer makes clear how much she loves the product you sell but she cannot get to your price. She wants to buy but you must 'help' her to do so. If done well, the Krunch works, and you slice your price in some way. Because the red player assumes as an article of faith that there is slack in every seller's prices, the Krunch is meant to reveal that slack in the nicest possible way. The seller invariably cuts the price or reveals other ways of reducing the buyer's costs, which confirms the belief that they pad prices.

Activity 11.5

Have you been the victim of a Krunch? Think of the circumstances
and recount how you felt and what made you comply.

Have you *used* the Krunch? How did the other party react?

The Killer has a similar intention. It asks, 'Is that the best you can
do?' Think of the impact on a beleaguered seller. They want the
business but must move on price to get it. So they do, which
justifies the buyer springing the killer line.

However, asking some Killer questions can provoke an unintended deadlock, as when you are asked whether 'that is your final
offer?' How do you answer that? If you say 'yes', then you fear that
the negotiation is over and you force them to take it or leave it; if
you say 'no', then you invite the next question: 'Well what *is* your
final offer?'

Of the Nibble, there is not much you can say to justify it. It is
pure-red play and is the largest single cause of a relationship
grinding to a stop. In the Nibble the other negotiator trims on the
details of what you thought you had agreed. For instance, the
deal was for 30 days credit, they take 40 days; it was for returns
within 7 days of delivery, so they send back returns in 11 days; it
was for deliveries in multiple gross amounts, and they supply
short measures of a few units per gross, and so on, right through
the list.

Nibbling is also common in long-running contracts when the
parties become too routine in their relationship and standards slip
– the courtship phase is inevitably followed by the cooling of
ardour. But nibbling, when it is intentional from the start, is pure
red play.

Activity 11.6

Do you nibble? Justify your behaviour. How is the other party
reacting to your nibbles?

Another red ploy is to present you with two unpleasant
alternatives, one so horrendous that you feel forced to choose the
less horrendous one. I call this ploy the 'Russian Front' – as in 'do

this or I'll send you to the Russian Front!' It is not easy to counter it if you believe the threat is credible. For example, accountancy firms up until recently were near-terrorised by Financial Directors telling them to 'cut your audit fees or we go out to tender'. And it is often used to stop slackness in an ongoing service contract appearing from unintentional nibbling: 'Restore fully the original standard of service or we ask your competitors for bids.'

Activity 11.7

When were you recently 'Russian Fronted'? Which option did you choose, and why?

Expectations can change dramatically in a business sector, so what was normal a few years ago suddenly becomes laughingly impossible to contemplate. These may be caused by external circumstances outside the control of the parties. Thus annual bonuses of a million pounds for London financiers have become the norm against which those in the sector judge their performance; football players who earn in a week the annual salary of their managers set targets for young hopefuls, who fall for the 'sell cheap, get famous' ploy (which explains the proliferation of footballers' agents hired to counter it); and entry prices for acquiring certain businesses now start at huge premiums, with 'crazy' multiples of a company's earnings being the norm.

Activity 11.8

In what ways has your business sector changed in recent years? Have the numbers got astronomically larger, or much less?

Knowing your business and understanding the changes in it will help you to negotiate. Yet negotiating these feverish games is a challenge for anybody mesmerised by strings of zeroes placed after an already unusually large number. Aggressively minded red players are at home in this environment, which makes them even more aggressive when they chase, and catch, the big numbers.

➡ STATEMENTS AS A TOOL

To protect your interests from red assaults on your perceptions, you need a simple behavioural tool (simple in its execution, that is) to add to those of questioning, summarising and signalling. You need this tool for you to survive long enough to exchange proposals and to avoid you completely crumbling under vigorous pressure from excited red players who sense they have got your measure.

To put the tool in context, the most common activity during negotiation is a host of behaviours I collect together and call 'statements'. Statements are neutral in that they are not directly argumentative (although red players react by arguing), nor are they the same as the behaviours of questioning, summarising or signalling found in constructive debate. Statements do not push the negotiation forward nor drag it backwards but, nevertheless, they play a major role in the discourse.

Surprisingly, statements often pass unnoticed as negotiation tools, yet they take up much of the time in negotiation. Being neutral, statements are made unemotionally – in contrast to more active debate behaviours.

You make statements when you explain what you want, when you answer questions, or when you make a supporting case for your general position on an issue. They are scene-setters and mostly you tend to tread carefully while you make them, using measured tones. Statements are not expressions of why you have differences, but are pure descriptions of your approach to the issues – *before* you explain why you disagree. You should make statements without commenting on the listener's alleged motivations or their intentions, because that provokes argumentative rebuttal or denial. Think of them as being descriptive in their scope rather than deliberately prejudicial.

Impatient red players, keen to get stuck in and mix it in argument, or blue players, wishing to leave argument behind and get on with something constructive, often pay no attention to the use of statements. Yet, they can repair cracks in confidence.

Activity 11.9

What do the following sentences have in common?

Unless we make a profit, we cannot support our customers when they are in difficulty.

If we are to accede to a price increase, we have to be convinced that it is unavoidable.

We can only accept practices that meet the highest ethical standards.

We can work with you in this project as long as it does not inhibit us from working with others.

I can agree to a non-exclusive agency but I cannot award exclusivity under European competition law.

In answer to the question in Activity 11.9, they are all statements from negotiation that defused red pressure.

Statements express interests

In making statements, you report on those aspects of your preparation that pertain to your interests. Remember that your interests are the best antidote to red pressure, and their exposition in the form of statements casts the negotiable issues as the servants of your interests and not the other way round.

For example, opponents of construction projects (new airport runways, new roads, new bridges, new shopping malls, and such like) take stances that usually fail in their objectives. They fight the projects on a yes–no dimension ('Yes, the projects will be built,' say the authorities; 'Oh, no they won't,' say the protestors). Wasting public money fighting on this dimension reduces the amount spent addressing the protestors' interests.

Activity 11.10

What are the interests of the individuals and groups who oppose the types of project just listed? (Hint: think of what their motives might be and how the projects make them personally worse off.)

Any listing of the opposers' interests would feature the preventing of knock-on effects such as pollution, noise, disamenities, reductions in property values, damage to the environment, and accidents. Staking everything on stopping a large project is certainly spectacularly ambitious, but the opposers should perhaps concentrate more on addressing their interests by negotiating adequate countermeasures to the project's disamenities. This would be a more useful strategy when the project goes ahead, even if less spectacular than trying to stop it.

I recommend an open mind, or at least a flexible approach, to a set of negotiable issues becoming the agenda. But remember, issues only have validity if they deliver your interests. So, under red pressure over negotiable issues, revert to making statements about your interests:

> We apply the principle that employers have a right to manage their enterprises and unions have a right to exercise their functions.

> Let me make it clear that we have a right to be paid for all of the services we supply and you have the right to pay only for the services that you receive.

> I do not really mind which security system you use at your premises, but whichever one is adopted it must treat visitors with respect and not with unnecessary suspicions. And it must not impose unreasonable delays that hurt our business.

> Your contentions over the royalty rate we charge appear to challenge our right to charge royalties for your use of our intellectual property.

> You seem to be saying that we cannot change our distributors and agents to suit our commercial interests unless we receive the permission of our competitors.

> While we accept that this person's conduct appears to be unacceptable, we cannot accept a situation where uncorroborated allegations constitute sufficient grounds in themselves to dismiss her.

> We cannot put anything in this contract that offends the laws of the host country or our own.

We must find another way to handle this option problem other than giving you the right of 'first refusal', because that effectively prevents us from legitimately negotiating with others in good faith.

Get the idea? Look for the principle behind what they want and contrast it with your interests.

Activity 11.11

Suppose one of your clients tells you that they want you to reduce your prices on some low-margin products, and they give as the main reason their need to reduce their costs. How might you compose a response as a statement? (Hint: consider prudent principles of financial solvency – for both parties.)

Recently, I negotiated with some people from a high-inflation economy, where the government imposed high taxes on employees and yet these people admitted that they voted for that government to be in power. They vigorously insisted that my client raise their wages to compensate them for their economy's rampant inflation and their high taxes. Setting aside their red tone and manners, I stated that in a democracy you get what you vote for and that my client was in the microchip and not the subsidy-for-high-taxes business. Their red pressure collapsed and later, when we returned to the wages issue, it was within a negotiated package of productivity measures that paid for itself.

Making statements has considerable merit when you are under red pressure. Red players prepare for negotiation with inordinate attention to the arguments that support their positions. They invest their emotional capital in expressing themselves in a manner designed to demonstrate their heavy commitment to what they want. They try to breach your defences by rhetoric.

But statements help you resist being bamboozled by rhetoric. They give you time to think: 'Hey, wait a minute! What is the principle they are trying to push me into accepting?' As always, the best people to enunciate their principles are themselves – so ask them to do so and state your own too. It sure beats red shaping power-plays.

For your toolkit

T11.1 Understand that the purpose of red ploys is to influence your perceptions of red players' power over you and thus to lower your expectations of the outcome of the negotiations.

T11.2 Realise that your perceptions of the power balance are in your head and may not correspond to reality.

T11.3 Watch out for variations of the tough-guy/soft-guy ploy. Identify solo versions of the tough-guy/soft-guy ploy and neutralise them.

T11.4 Prepare for the Krunch by realising that the other party may use it no matter what you offer.

T11.5 Counter the Killer with: 'I am always willing to consider suggestions that will increase the acceptability of my proposals.' Then shut up and let them make the suggestions.

T11.6 To counter Nibbles, react to them when they first appear and insist that they abide with the terms of the agreement. Punish persistent nibbling by taking your business elsewhere.

T11.7 Do not nibble, intentionally or otherwise.

T11.8 Identify a Russian Front ploy and judge its credibility before responding. It is a red ploy and indicates you may need to reconsider the relationship with the other party.

T11.9 Select and use statements of your interests to defuse red behaviour and ploys.

T11.10 Practise devising summary stance statements to deflect power ploys from playing on your expectations.

T11.11 Use stances to project your commitment.

Chapter 12
In praise of purple

➡ DICK WHITTINGTON'S CAT

We now come to the crux of negotiating behaviour, namely the resolution of the red–blue dilemma, or when to overcome the risk of trust. For, make no mistake: without trust, business would be extremely primitive. Therefore, we should not be surprised that it took many millennia for social mechanisms to evolve in business so as to ensure trust. The risks were too high for trust to spread easily (and are still too high in many poverty-stricken countries).

Consider the children's fable of Dick Whittington and his cat, and what it tells us about trust in trade. If you remember the story, some London merchant venturers put together a cargo to ship to Siam and make them all rich. The already rich merchants put all kinds of luxuries into the ship to trade with the King of Siam, but all Dick possessed was a cat, so his contribution to the venture was somewhat modest. The ship eventually returned with spices, gold, silver, rubies and diamonds from the King in exchange for the 'luxury' goods sent by the merchants. For Dick there was a special bonus. The King was so pleased with Dick's cat, because it chased and killed all the rats that overran his palace, that he sent to him boxes of precious stones to make him rich beyond the dreams of avarice.

A good story, and it tells you something about trade that is not obvious.

Activity 12.1

What does the fable of Dick Whittington tell you about trade and trust? (Hint: how long was a voyage to Siam in the seventeenth century?)

It took many voyages to develop a workable international trading system that reduced the risk of trust. The natural elements of wind, water and unfriendly shores were ever ready to destroy flimsy craft sailing over long distances. But the proclivities of humans to defect were of greater danger to the success of such voyages than the neutral natural elements.

How could the merchant venturers, once the captain of their vessel was out of their sight, be sure that he would not turn left for France instead of heading for Siam? In France, he could sell their cargo and live in luxury, without risking a long and dangerous voyage to Siam and back. Of course, if this had happened in the story of Dick Whittington, Lord Mayor of London, it would not have had its happy ending (though I often wonder what happened to his cat). But if piratical behaviour became the norm, few would have risked their capital in funding such ventures, and international trade would have been stifled at birth.

➡ REDUCING THE RISK OF TRUST

The merchant venturers minimised their individual risks of natural disasters and of defecting crews by each contributing only a small affordable proportion of the total value of the cargo at risk. They risked a small loss for a share in the large cargo assembled for the voyage, which if successful would make them a huge gain. Much the same idea eventually produced the limited-liability joint stock companies of the nineteenth century.

Activity 12.2

Reconsider Jake's parable on trust from Chapter 6 and see if you can devise a way for him to minimise his risks of losing $100 by a scheme like that used by the merchant venturers to minimise their individual risks.

Wherever communities have been unable to discover ways of minimising the risk of trust – as, for example, in the south of Italy and Sicily, and parts of the Third World – economic development is stifled. Add institutionalised corruption and the grasping greed of local oligarchies (criminal or legitimate), and their economic failure is fully explained.

Painfully and slowly, the prohibitive risk of trust was reduced historically by individuals spreading their risks across many voyages until the gross value of international trade eventually flourished into unprecedented amounts. The defectors (who are always with us) gradually became the minority and were replaced by a majority of trustworthy co-operators. Indeed, potential defectors came to keep their promises because of the draconian and impersonal consequences for those who defected from them. They hanged pirates, didn't they?

Once bloody retribution was at least probable for defectors, be they pirates, mutineers, fraudsters, thieves, corrupt officials or opportunist crooks, their numbers declined sufficiently for honest and trusting trade to expand peacefully. And expand it did, at first only marginally faster than the economic damage caused by defectors, but that was all that was needed for honest (enough) trade to become dominant over time.

Don't make the mistake of thinking of traders being saints. On a personal level there may not have been much to differentiate them from crooks, fraudsters and rogues – and some of them traded in slaves. But the social rewards of honest trade far exceeded the relatively puny rewards of dishonest individuals. Most pirates, for example, apparently murderously fell upon each other while hiding in remote enclaves, which were far from places where their plundered riches could be gainfully invested.

Meanwhile, the world's trading system became an all-pervasive presence across vast types and quantities of commodities. The reinvestment of the profits, through the power of compound interest, ensured steady economic growth on scales unimaginable in previous epochs.

Activity 12.3

Do you know how to estimate the doubling time of any given amount from its growth rate? Simply divide 74 by the growth rate (expressed as a percentage). This assumes that the growth is added to the total and that new total grows at the same rate, and so on for each year, until the original quantity is doubled.

How long would it take your country's GNP to double in size if its annual growth rate was 1%? Try it now for several different growth rates.

If an economy grows at 3% it doubles in size in 25 years; at 5% it doubles in 14.8 years; at 7.5% it doubles in just under ten years; and so on. Steady growth of nearly 3% (roughly the UK norm for 150 years) ensures a doubling of the Gross National Product every 24 years. Nothing spectacular, perhaps, compared with recent Asian growth rates, but in this 'race', steady is best because it is relentless.

It is not accidental, in my view, that many early trading ventures were run by members of the same family. Families intimately know the degree of trustworthiness of each family member and it doesn't take much intelligence to match business tasks to the known reliability of each of them. Trusting strangers is more problematical.

If these small family businesses remain corralled in their distrust of strangers and non-family members, they remain small and suffer intergenerational attrition (which is expressed well in the wry comment 'clogs to clogs in three generations'). In some parts of the world (southern Italy is the classic case), people in a single village do not trust each other, never mind those from another village, and they remain desperately poor as a result.

Where the rule of law governs trading relations, and people combine their efforts into large-scale production sequences that are driven by vast divisions of labour, economic vitality is assured. The employees in these markets are virtual strangers, unrelated by family, clan, nationality or religion. Indeed, where such relations are important, markets become distorted and the participants are poorer.

Activity 12.4

Can you explain why excluding dealings with persons outside the family, clan, nation, ethnic or religious group makes people less wealthy than they could be?

People and trust

In theory, people in markets are anonymously dependent on each other, and their products can be bought and sold impersonally without any person having to know the identities of anybody else in the chain of transactions. In this case, the focus is mainly on the product and not the person buying or selling it. Take people out of the equation and the risk of trust reduces to the reputation of the product (for example, its brand name).

Trust comes back into this idealised picture because trade is conducted by people acting either as a buyer or a seller. You don't buy a PC from Compaq but from someone selling it on behalf of Compaq, and similarly (in general) for all other products.

How then does the pressure to reduce the risk of trust express itself in negotiating behaviour? In a most interesting yet ultimately simple way. Markets are operated by people, and people bring to their activities their red and blue attitudes. That is an inescapable factor in understanding the successful mediation of risk and trust. The red player treats everybody as a stranger; the blue player treats everybody as a friend. What they have in common is a lack of reliable evidence for according either status to the people with whom they negotiate.

In low-trust encounters (for example, in Italian villages riven by universal suspicion of everybody by everybody) a stranger represents an ill-defined threat and is treated in a hostile manner. Red play in negotiation replicates hostile behaviour appropriate for low-trust encounters. In contrast, in high-trust encounters (for example, within a closely knit family business) a friend represents someone who is not a threat to the interests of the family. Blue play therefore provides friendly behaviour appropriate for high-trust encounters.

Neither red nor blue behaviour is appropriate as a strategy for negotiation in a market, because it is not true that all strangers threaten one's interests nor that all friends benignly protect them. These primitive stereotypes that drive red or blue players become behavioural culs-de-sac. Mainly, they usually result in suboptimal deals for both parties.

Activity 12.5

Think of reasons why this should be so. What is it in the behaviour of red or blue players that produces suboptimal deals over time?

Dead ends of red and blue

The red player seeks to take as much as she can from the transaction: 'Give me this, give me that.' She intends to give as little as possible away and to get as much as possible from you. Her behaviour is as hostile to your interests as it is benign towards her own. Negotiators who realise they have been treated unfairly become suspicious in these circumstances of the intentions of those they deal with, and in future they reduce their risks of further losses by curbing their exposure.

The blue player seeks to give as much as she can to protect the relationship: 'Take this, take that.' She is willing to exchange as much as possible from her for as little as is necessary from you. Her behaviour is as benign to your interests as it is self-sacrificing towards her own. Negotiators who realise they have been overgenerous in their treatment of others, because the latter do not reciprocate as expected, are less generous in future. They too curb their exposure (or they run out of the resources with which to practise their generosity if, eventually, they do not curb their blue behaviour).

➡ PURPLE BEHAVIOUR

The analogy I have long used to illustrate the dead ends of the separate behaviours of red and blue is that of the elements of sodium and chlorine. Ingested by themselves, sodium and chlorine are hostile to your health, and in large dosages they can kill you.

Yet, your body cannot survive for long without regularly ingesting both of these elements. This is achieved by the ingenious solution of providing them both via regular dosages of common table salt (sodium chloride).

Similarly, social evolution provides you with an ingenious solution to the dead ends of choosing between red or blue behaviour. Don't separate them, join them!

What is a red demand but the expression of wanting something for nothing? As a child, adults were the source of everything you wanted. As an adult you know you have in fact no bottomless pits in your gift. What is a blue offer but the expression of you giving something for nothing? As a parent, your child is the object of your love and affection, upon whom you pour everything within your gift that is good for them. If you had a bottomless pit of goodies, it would never contain enough for you to give them lovingly to your child (but as an adult you know that may not be in the child's best interests but, as bottomless pits are fantasies, you do them no harm in striking attitudes commensurate with the wish).

The negotiator neither takes (red) nor gives (blue) as separate acts. The negotiator combines red taking with blue giving into the purple conditional principle behind all acts of trading: 'If you give me some of what I want, then I will give you some of what you want.' In this format, the red demand ('some of what I want') is linked inextricably to the blue offer ('some of what you want') and, as long as they are linked, no amount of red play or red deviousness can ambush the purple proposal.

If–Then

Note the format: 'If ..., then ...'. Those familiar with computer programming will immediately recognise the basic imperative of the program: 'If X, then Y'. It has no room for ambiguity. Y only happens if X occurs. Anything less than X does not produce anything like Y. Hence, the assertion that 'you will get absolutely nothing from me unless and until I get something from you' states the absolute imperative of all purple negotiators. This is a trade, not a one-way red street nor a one-way blue give-away.

Those negotiators who hit on this format by accident or design always do better than those who fumble into some other format. Apart from variations in the wording used ('provided that', 'with the proviso' or 'on condition that', or something similar), all other attempts to circumvent the purple conditionality principle of 'if–then' are doomed to failure. Negotiators end up, instead, reverting to red or blue behaviour.

It is not unusual for practitioners to question my assertion that the format of if–then gives them total protection from lapsing into red or blue behaviour. Some have been amazed to discover that the solution can be so simply expressed. They look for a complex solution to a simple problem. They forget what negotiation is about: you exchange something you have for something you want.

What better way is there than to express this simple notion in the form of a purple conditional if–then proposal? The key lies in its assertive conditionality. Its assertiveness is in the red demand for you to be given what you want as the only way in which you will make the blue offer to give them what they want. They can't get your blue offer without meeting your red demand!

This is the real toughness of a negotiator. It does not rely on threats or abuse or any of the red manners displayed by red players. A quiet determination to trade thwarts one-sided red demands. Red players must consider the content of the exchange if they want something from you, because there is no other way they are going to get anything they want.

Activity 12.6

How should you treat openly-soft blue players? Is there anything you can do to alter their behaviour? Should you resign yourself to having to take advantage of them?

Is it only your responsibility to apply purple conditionality to red players?

I recommend that you treat openly-soft blue players the same as you treat red players, only in reverse. You are not out to exploit anybody, even when negotiating with soft blues. You formulate all of your proposals, and reformulate their give-aways, in the same if–then manner. If they have not specified what return for their free gifts, you tell them what they will

This sometimes causes doubtful looks in those who bemoan the red behaviours of others, as if their inclina take the free gifts from soft blues without exchanging a return. In other words, they seem inclined to play red i get away with it! The purple negotiator, however, serves another more general social purpose than individually exploiting blue players, namely that of reducing the number of free-gift blue players, for blue players who by their unconditional actions reward red play thereby encourage red play to replicate.

Every time you show a soft blue player the purple key to them ceasing to be a victim of red play, you reduce the scope for successful red play by reducing the number of people who choose to play blue because they do not know how to play anything else. Your trading actions show them the alternative. Long-term self-interest mandates you to practise unselfish purple play.

Activity 12.7

Suppose a blue player says: 'OK, I'll give you a 10% discount' and asks for nothing in return. How would you respond, if you wanted to show them how to trade? (Hint: reformulate their free gift discount by linking it to something you want or by asking a question.)

Purple play is robust. It stands up to all other versions of negotiating behaviour. Combined with the refusal to react to another player's behaviour, no matter how extreme its redness, purple play is never intimidatory; it never initiates defection; and it always sets out the solution to the negotiated problem in the conditional-exchange format.

Devious reds, who hide their intentions and against whom you have no defence using traditional red or blue means, are powerless against the purple conditional format. A condition is exactly that, and unless devious reds meet the condition by addressing your wants, there is no way they can take what you offer. 'No condition, no offer' flummoxes them. They have no means of disarming what they are up against because all their wiles are impotent in the face of your purple determination.

MULTI–ISSUE NEGOTIATIONS

Multi-issue negotiation is perfect for purple conditionality. The single-issue haggle is not the norm, except when you fall into the trap of separating the issues until you only have one left to settle (usually the money). In most negotiations, however, you must settle a multitude of issues. It does not have to become a zero-sum contest, and there is much to recommend you preventing it from becoming one.

In a single-issue contest, any movement by you towards the other party worsens your position and improves theirs; your loss is their gain. But in most negotiations there is more than one negotiable issue. Even a single issue like the money contains within it many subissues. The amount of money is one issue, when the money is paid is another, and how it is paid and through whom are others. Similar issues and subissues can be derived for other negotiable issues.

I call these the tradables of the deal, and it is your job as a negotiator to identify as many tradables in a deal as you can find. The more tradables, the greater your potential for flexibility. By varying individual tradables, a deal can be put together that fits more closely a negotiator's needs, and this increases the chances of its acceptability.

Take a simple bank loan as an example. The main negotiable issues are the amount of the loan, the security for the loan, the interest rate on the borrowing, and the duration of the loan. A quick scan of these negotiable issues produces the following, but by no means exhaustive, list of tradables for each of them:

- The amount of the loan can consist of several parts: the total amount, how it is subdivided and in what proportions; and when it may be drawn down and under what conditions (architect's certificates, completion notes, etc.).

- Security can take many forms: a pledge of the borrower's assets against the loan can consist of heritable property (whose valuation?), cash reserves (minimum balances?), cash flows (through what accounts?), goods, chattels and artefacts (where are they to be kept for safe-keeping), and shares, bonds and financial assets, like life insurance, pensions, etc.

- Interest (how much over base rates?) on the borrowing can include: capital or interest 'holidays' (for how long?); fees to put the loan together; balloon repayments; rolled-up amounts; consolidation packages; and early repayment penalties.

- Duration is as divisible as there are days and years in the calendar.

Activity 12.8

What are the tradables in your current negotiation? Pick one typical negotiation and prepare a list of tradables – all those items over which you and the other party have discretion. If something can be varied in any way, then potentially it is a tradable.

The negotiable issues are linked, in that some depend on each other. Duration is influenced by the types of security available – for example, pledging the rent from a 25-year tight lease with a blue-chip tenant can easily cover a loan of long duration, whereas a three-year rental stream from a shaky client is not so convincing.

But linking issues in the negotiation is not confined to natural relationships, such as security and duration of a loan. There is no reason why negotiators need restrict themselves in such a manner, and very good reasons for *not* doing so. Trading across several unrelated issues has advantages. A purple negotiator may propose movement on one or more issues in exchange for movement on unrelated others by linking them conditionally. This can be persuasive where a negotiator feels that what they lose on this issue is compensated by what they gain on the others.

This turns zero-sum movements into non-zero-sum movements. The log jam breaks as each party considers the net gains over the losses from movement across the issues, including the tradables within each main issue. This is very different from the certain (and psychic) loss negotiators feel when considering movement on a single issue only.

Conditionality smoothes the process by which net gains are realised. It is a powerful tool in your repertoire and fully occupies our attention in the middle (proposing) and the closing (bargaining) phases of the negotiation.

For your toolkit

T12.1 Reduce the risk of trust by breaking down each risk into smaller ones.

T12.2 Match responsibilities for risky tasks to individuals of known levels of trustworthiness.

T12.3 Always combine your red demands with your blue offers.

T12.4 Always (no exceptions!) formulate proposals in the if–then format ('If ..., then ...).

T12.5 Think 'purple conditionality'.

T12.6 Nobody gets anything from you unless and until you get something from them.

T12.7 Counter open intimidation and potential deviousness by insisting on if–then linking of demands to offers.

T12.8 Link issues and avoid zero-sum choices.

T12.9 Identify the discretionary tradables in your business.

Chapter 13
Proposing: your commitment to consider

➡ **SIGNALLING AND PROPOSING**

There is some controversy about where signalling ends and proposing begins, but classification controversies sometimes miss the point. The labels 'signalling' and 'proposing' are useful as first-order organising concepts but not as rigidly defined absolutes.

Signalling is observable (though not always observed). By their nature – the switch from absolute to relative statements – signals are tentative hints rather than fog-horn noises. If you do not listen, you miss them. Your hearing can be in the 'off' mode for the precise second it takes them to say 'difficult' in place of 'impossible'. Oblivious is as oblivious does.

Proposing behaviour is tentative, if markedly less tentative than signals. And the many shades of tentativeness between absolute tentativeness and relative tentativeness are the main cause of people indulging in esoteric debates on when one behaviour transforms into another.

➡ **PROPOSING BEHAVIOUR**

So the time has come to explore the behaviours known as 'proposing', their nature and purpose and how you can propose to powerful effect. I distinguish proposing behaviour from sending proposals to the other side, as when you price a specification, make a claim, or respond to a request for a proposal (known as 'RFP' in the jargon). These proposals have formats and styles, distinctively different from the behaviour of proposing.

Activity 13.1

What is absent in the following form of proposing?

How about if I made it £500 instead of £540?

OK. I'll throw in the gloves and the goggles.

I couldn't go as low as £20,000.

The one thing that is missing, of course, in each case is the immediately preceding dialogue that accompanied each statement, and the absence distorts your ability to identify the merits of the statements. You will agree, I presume, that the three statements plausibly conform to those found in a typical negotiating discourse. And you would be right, because the majority of negotiators are not immune from making mistakes while proposing. However, my assertion is that these fairly typical types of statement are examples of *serious* behavioural mistakes and their correction initially requires some work.

None of them is in the mandatory purple format; that is your first clue. Proposing in anything but the purple format is an avoidable mistake.

The first statement is a question: 'How about if I made it £500 instead of £540?' That is its first mistake. Proposals that ask questions are unassertive because they ask permission and, as the Jesuits advise, 'it is better to seek forgiveness than permission'. To ask the other negotiator if this or that is acceptable is to invite them to decline: 'I would love to say "yes" but unfortunately I can't.' Even a blue player could manage that, while for a red player they would do it in autopilot. What do you require in return for moving your price by 7% or so? Nothing? You cannot be serious. Something? Then why have you not linked what you want to what you give, as purple behaviour requires?

The two remaining examples are statements not questions and they are all the more robust for that. But they are also examples of concessionary, not trading, behaviour. To say 'I'll throw in the gloves and the goggles' is to make a one-way concession. Saying 'throw in' suggests in itself that you consider items of low priority to you are not worth much to the listener. And if you 'couldn't go as low as £20,000', I would feel obliged to ask you, 'How low could you go?' As a signal it might work, but as a proposal it does not.

Signalling is different from proposing because a signal is about creating 'safe' conditions for the possibilities of movement without initiating a slide to surrender, while proposing tentatively suggests possible trades for consideration.

The language of proposing

The language of proposing advertises its purpose because proposing behaviours, when expressed in the purple format, consist of two elements, the red condition (what you want) and the blue offer (what they get).

Now, the order is important: the condition precedes the offer. You tell them what they must do if they are to get what you offer, that is, you put the condition before the offer (C + O).

Activity 13.2

To test your understanding, rearrange the (correct) C + O format of the following proposal into an (incorrect) O + C format: 'If you would reconsider the definition of "the Territory", then I would consider a longer licence period.' (Hint: think about what placing the offer before the condition invites from the listener. OK, this is difficult, so to make it easier, I will write the first part of the O + C format, and you fill in the wording of the second part: 'If I consider a longer licensing period, ...'.)

Presumably, the one thing you did – or were certainly tempted to do – was to restate the proposal as a question ('If I consider a longer licence period, would you reconsider the definition of "the Territory"?'). That this is difficult to avoid is proven in practice by the number of negotiators who lead with the offer followed by the conditon (i.e., 'If I ..., will you ...?'). You almost cannot help a question if you state your offer first. You will save the effort required to avoid a question by formatting your proposal correctly as C + O.

Offer-first proposing is partly attitudinal: you do not want to come across as excessively aggressive in tone. That you have come this far in becoming aware of the need for purple conditionally is a big step. But hesitating in mid-stride is uncomfortable, and importing blue timidity into your new behaviour is not the answer.

Negotiators coached to avoid red tones and behaviours often overcompensate and act ultra-polite, but they usually revert when they address issues closer to their interests – it is easier to be polite and considerate when issues do not threaten interests. But the greatest danger for you is to entrench fallacious behaviours during temporary blue relapses, and to allow these to remain uncorrected when you revert to redder behaviours.

A defensive explanation for habitually proposing in the O + C format usually slides into weary pleas, from those who feel harried by a tutor's corrections, of 'does it matter all that much?' Yes, it does matter – or more correctly, the attitudinal impulses causing it matter.

Of course, blue players wrap their language in softer words and express it in softer tones, and introducing them to the conditional proposal in an if–then format is uncomfortable. Red players, coming at it from a different angle and conscious of their tendency to demand without making offers, also try to tone down and use softer language. Unassertive words such as 'like', 'wish' and 'hope' become overused. Unacceptable proposals, instead of receiving summary red rejections, are described as 'a wee bit more than we can afford', 'a trifle too high', and 'not quite what we had in mind', even when, in truth, 'wee', 'trifle' and 'not quite' do not describe the seriousness of their rejections.

Assertive behaviour is not red behaviour to any degree. Red players assert their rights but ignore the rights of others; purple players assert their rights and acknowledge that others have rights too. The difference can be expressed in language and tone, but it is more than one of mere presentation. The assertive conditional proposal in the 'If you ..., then I ... ' format is not aggressive either in language or tone. It does not ignore or deny the rights of others but states the connection openly and clearly: if you address my rights in this manner then I will address your rights in that manner. It is in no way all take or all give because it joins taking and giving into a single and clearly stated sentence.

The words used are 'require', 'need', and 'must have' rather than 'like', 'hope' and 'wish'. The clarity of the former set means they are not aggressive because they state clearly the nature of the transaction. The 'nicer' vagueness of the latter set invite misinterpretations of one's commitment, which is in nobody's interests in the serious business of negotiation and can be positively dangerous when negotiating in a totally red climate. When red players misjudge your commitment because you use language and formats that hide it, the outcome can become messy or, worse, bloody.

Hence, build in the C + O format from the beginning, and never vary it. You will become proficient with practice in saying what you mean and meaning what you say, and the people with whom you negotiate will not think any the less of you for your assertiveness.

Making tentative suggestions

Proposing is about being tentative. It is not something you learn from books or training courses. Negotiators beginning the process of movement universally do so tentatively at first. Their caution is explicable by the natural hesitation against moving decisively in large steps in case they move farther than they need to or intend.

Even in auctions, bidders move in small steps, except when the serious bidders sometimes move in large steps to shake out the minnows before stalking a serious rival. An extraordinarily large bid near the end of an auction can eliminate the field in one swipe, but the bidder will almost certainly pay too much.

Hence, you learn tentative proposal behaviour socially and not from trainers. Your first experiences of tentative suggestions are when you feel shy about making them – and what school for learning to make tentative suggestions beats that of your first fumbles at courtship! Training then imparts economical ways of making tentative suggestions to support what you learned from social intercourse. And the most telling of these fits neatly into the purple format of if–then.

A word like 'consider' summarises the tentative imperatives of proposing. In exchange for what you require them to do, you will 'consider' what you will do for them. Synonyms for consider have their role, of course, but for simplicity let me stick with that one word.

Activity 13.3

What other words could you use in place of 'consider' without losing its essential tentativeness?

While it is necessary for you always to be vague about the outcome of your commitment to consider what they want, you may be as vague or as specific as is convenient about what you require of them. It makes sense to be vague about both the condition and the offer in the earlier stages of the making of tentative suggestions.

An early very tentative proposal could take the form: 'If you consider my wants, then I could consider yours.' This could be followed later by a less tentative proposal in the form: 'If you agree to pay for my full R&D costs, then I will consider your application for a licence to use my patents.' In the first sentence, both the condition and the offer are vague; you only require them to consider your wants and in return you could consider theirs. In the second sentence, you require them to agree to your specific requirement, namely 'to pay my full R&D costs', for which you vaguely agree to consider their application for a licence.

You require the other party to commit but you do not (yet) offer to commit yourself. In other words, you are still in the proposing phase. Beware of confusing proposals and offers: in proposing, a condition may be vague or specific, but an offer is *always* vague. That is how you recognise a proposal – by its vagueness in the offer.

Activity 13.4

What are the errors in the following proposals?

If you consider my requirements, then I will increase my offer by 10%.

If I increase my offer by 10%, will you reconsider your rejection of my requirements?

OK, a 10% discount – but only for a bigger order.

Again, defending sloppy language betrays ignorance of the distinctive role of proposing behaviour. In all three cases, the offer is specific and the condition is vague, making them sloppy and less effective than assertive proposals. On such a distinction rides your effectiveness as a negotiator.

Negotiating is seldom neat and tidy and proposal behaviour may be exhibited at any moment. Truly, however, nothing much happens in negotiating until somebody makes proposals. You cannot negotiate arguments, opinions, assertions, allegations, imputations, attacks, threats, beliefs or principles. There are two solutions for every problem – yours and theirs – and for as long as only the opening solutions remain, debate consists largely of verbiage, interspersed with shorter and ruder ways of saying 'no!'

➡ RESPONDING TO PROPOSING BEHAVIOUR

Proposing behaviour can occur at any time and you want tools to respond to it. The general position must be that proposing behaviour, like signalling, is best encouraged by a positive response. Proposing manifests the movement implied in the signal. And proposing behaviour in the assertive format, and consisting of a vague or specific condition but always with a vague offer, lends itself to a positive response.

Activity 13.5

Of two ways of responding to a given proposal by you, which would you find the most encouraging?

- If they said 'No'.
- If they said 'Yes'.

Saying 'No' is a show stopper. On its own, and particularly when accompanied by rhetorical flourishes or (worse) expletives, an instant rejection is dispiriting. It does not discriminate between that part of the proposal that might be acceptable, albeit with some amendments, and that part that is absolutely beyond consideration. If everything in a proposal is absolutely beyond the pale, there is not much room for them to move, and probably little incentive for them to do so.

Saying 'Yes' is also a show stopper, if of a different sort. To what are you saying 'Yes'? Maybe you were not listening too well (a not uncommon occurrence) and you missed the vagueness of their offer? Or, they sloppily got it round the wrong way and made it a vague condition accompanied by a specific offer (also not uncommon). Whichever it was, your 'Yes' response is a problem.

With proposals you still have work to do which is why they are vague in the offer. A vague offer that is made almost without prompting invites questions, and that is your best response. What do they mean by this or that aspect of their offer? In short, what does 'consider' mean for you?

You may also question the condition and its vague or specific content. You should question the proposal to make sure that you understand it before you respond with your considered comments.

So neither 'No' nor 'Yes' is a helpful response. If, however, you receive either of these responses to *your* proposals, you have to move the debate on to more productive territory.

Activity 13.6

If you receive a firm 'No' to a given proposal of yours, would you say you were in a stronger or a weaker position than the other party?

The best response to a blanket 'No' is not to argue with them. You could ask why they rejected your proposal so firmly, and be prepared to listen for signals during their rejection. And after they say their piece – or without it if they refuse to tell you (not uncommon!) – you can say something to the effect: 'Well, I have made a proposal and you have rejected it out of hand. So what is your proposal?'

The maker of a rejected proposal, psychologically at least, is in a stronger position than the person who has not made a proposal at all. You do not have to make a second, third or fourth proposal, just because they reject everything you propose; indeed, I strongly caution you against making a new proposal in response to a rejection (or an outright silence) because such behaviour only incites them to keep rejecting your proposals without revealing their hand.

Proposals can be complex and cover many issues, or simple and only link one or two. Experience suggests that proposals are better for being unadorned with explanations. It is better to make your explanations before detailing your proposal. Flagging an intention to make a proposal, such as by saying something like 'Let me make a suggestion' is an attention grabber. It seldom fails to work and almost always provokes an attentive reaction. The more formal the style in which you make a proposal (in an if–then format, of course), the more likely it is to receive the close attention of those listening. Shambolic rambles are time-wasting, confusing and start off more hares than you have time to chase. That is why clearly listing your conditions helps them understand what you want, and clearly listing what could be in your offer does the same.

➡ SHUT UP!

Because silence isolates the proposal from corruption by non-relevant notions, after stating your proposal in an almost formal manner, my best advice is for you to shut up. You want the other party to concentrate on the content of what you propose and not the argumentative elements that might be provoked by explaining this or that feature.

Likewise, when hearing a proposal, shut up and let them – if they must – make the mistake of elaborating on the content. When you do speak it must be only to ask questions and to make sure you understand the content.

Activity 13 7

Practise 'shutting up' whenever you can. That means refraining from filling the silence with words, after you ask a question (don't elaborate on why you asked the question or what you expect them to answer!), after you make a statement, after you propose and after you bargain. You will do this most effectively by imposing a sudden silence immediately after a complete sentence. Try it during your next conversation.

Instantly reacting to the content, particularly to reject parts you do not properly understand, upsets the proposer because it implies that you have not given it sufficient consideration. In that way you miss a trick because one of the roles of the if–then format is to assure the other party of your commitment to consider their wants.

Questioning of the details and little diversionary debates usually accompanies the exchange of proposals, as the negotiators try to firm up the vagueness of the offers. In time, this behaviour leads on naturally to the specification of bargains, which usually closes the final phases of the negotiation.

For your toolkit

T13.1 Always state your proposals in the purple 'if–then' format.

T13.2 Always state your conditions first, followed by your offer (C + O).

T13.3 Avoid proposals that lead with your offer followed by your conditions in question form ('If I give you ..., will you ... ?').

T13.4 State your proposals in assertive language that is neither aggressive nor weak in wording or tone.

T13.5 In proposing, make tentative suggestions to address each party's wants.

T13.6 State the terms under which you will commit to 'consider' the other party's wants.

T13.7 Your condition may be vague or specific, but your offer to consider should always be vague.

T13.8 Require the other party to commit to your wants in exchange for you considering their wants.

T13.9 In responding to a proposal, avoid 'No' or 'Yes' because they are not effective and can be misleading.

T13.10 Question the condition and the offer of a proposal until you understand it.

T13.11 Always shut up after making a proposal.

Chapter 14
Bargaining: your commitment to trade

➡ NEGOTIATIONS HAVE EVENTUALLY TO END

Speak to well-seasoned professional negotiators and they recount tales of their seemingly endless and interminable negotiations. Happily, they only seem that way while you suffer them. Paraphrasing Sartre, you might well define 'Hell' as 'an endless negotiation with other people'.

Activity 14.1

Are you currently involved in some interminable negotiations that appear to have no obvious end point? How has this unhappy and uncomfortable situation arisen? Is it time to call a halt?

Fortunately, all negotiation processes eventually end, either in an agreement to disagree or an agreement to trade. If it does not matter when you conclude a specific negotiation, then there is not much point wasting your time negotiating that issue. Managers implement the decisions they negotiate, which requires that they eventually must end the negotiations.

The closing phase of negotiation is the formulation and the acceptance or rejection of the concluding bargain. I used to call the 'close' a separate behavioural step in the sequence, but I was hard put to demonstrate its content (following the edict to provide an example for every concept), and I came to the conclusion that there was nothing in the so-called 'close' that was essentially different from bargaining behaviour. True, negotiations open and negotiations close but identifying the specific behaviours of the opening and the close does not add much to understanding or performance.

➡ BARGAINING BEHAVIOUR

Use of the word 'bargain' is not a judgement on the quality of the deal – you can make lousy bargains. Bargaining is a behaviour. It consists of the terms for the agreement and takes a similar format to that of proposing, except that it is specific and not tentative. In proposing you make tentative suggestions of possible terms for a deal; in bargaining you make specific statements of the terms upon which you are prepared to settle.

Bargains are best expressed in the 'if–then' format, for example:

> If you accept the conditions I have specifed, then I will offer you
> a firm contract to buy the property outlined in green on this
> survey map for a price of $12 million.

Both the condition and the offer are specific. There is no room for ambiguity in the concluding bargain because if both parties agree to the bargain they live with whatever they sign and without whatever they do not specify.

The normal, though not mandatory, sequence from signal to the concluding bargain is one characterised by increasing specificity. Signals vaguely hint at a vague willingness to consider vague movement; early proposals are vague in both the condition and the offer; later proposals specify the condition but not the offer; early bargains specify both the condition and the offer and they reach their final conclusion in a bargain that is highly specific in all of its conditions and in all aspects of its offer.

Between each of these steps from vagueness to specificity there is much verbiage, debate, diversion and the revisiting of old ground. Neither party controls the conduct of the process. But strip out the to-ing and fro-ing that necessarily accompanies negotiation inter-actions and the essence of what goes on is revealed as the movement from the initial solutions the negotiators bring to the table, through the consideration of various degrees of vague alternative solutions and increasing specificity, to a concluded bargain that is specific in all of its elements.

Activity 14.2

Go over a recent negotiation and compare the initial proposals that the parties made and check through the various amending proposals that were exchanged.

How different was the final bargain to what had originally been proposed? Which party suggested which amendments? Can you recollect suggested amendments that were rejected or found to be unworkable in some way?

The 'if–then' format

In bargaining, the essential format of 'if–then' encapsulates the meaning of a negotiated solution and separates negotiation from all other forms of decision making. If–then reveals the social roots of negotiation in the bargain: 'If you give me what I want, then I will offer you so much of what you want.'

All my cautions that were introduced for the tools of the if–then format in proposing behaviour apply also in bargaining, only more so. You can recover from slips in proposing, but slips in bargaining language undermine your assertiveness (and, therefore, the other party's attentive commitment to addressing your interests) and have a disproportionately negative effect on the outcome. You must take care to state your specific conditions first, followed by your specific offer, and you must avoid leading with your offer followed by your conditions, as this is destined – as with the proposal – to become an unassertive question.

Activity 14.3

For preparatory practice, write down some possible bargains for a current negotiation in the if–then format, using a sheet of A4 paper and marking a column on the left as 'Conditions' and a column on the right as 'Offers'. Be specific in completing each column, linking conditions and offers on each of the issues.

Your bargaining statements identify your terms for the other party getting what they want, and if you speak with an uncertain voice they may conclude that your bargain is not close to your final word. Thus try to speak with directness and authority and, as with proposals and questions, shut up after stating your bargain. The silence is an effective attention grabber. In the bargain, you require them to commit to your wants in exchange for you committing to theirs. The bargain is, in effect, your 'price' for the deal.

➡ RESPONDING TO BARGAINING

How might you respond to a bargain? It is likely to be similarly to a proposal but with a significant behavioural difference in one respect.

Remember, you are not advised to respond to a proposal with a 'No' because it is too abrupt, it has negative red connotations and it suggests you are not committed, at least, to considering their wants, which is unhelpful in inducing them to consider yours. Effective responding behaviour includes anything that ensures you understand what they propose. Asking questions is an obvious means to use as your initial response, followed (when ready) with your alternative proposal or suggestions as to how to amend their proposal to make it more acceptable to you.

Activity 14.4

When did you last suffer a total rejection of a bargain, or totally reject a bargain offered to you? How did you feel when they just said 'No!'?

What happened next? Did the atmosphere change for the better or the worse?

And the difference in bargaining? You can respond fairly quickly to an offered bargain with a counter-bargain, without the negative implication that you are disregarding their wants. Why? Because closing bargains are detailed in both condition and offer and they usually follow considerable discussion of each side's proposals of how they want their interests addressed. If this is not the case, then you have not been paying attention to all that precedes the exchange of bargains!

It is an error to attempt to bargain before detailed discussion of the issues has taken place. Everything that precedes bargaining clears the way, so to speak, and reveals the choices starkly. You should then have a pretty clear idea of what is possible in the circumstances. Trying to bargain too early and before each party fully understands what each wants is unlikely to curtail the need for fuller discussions. Remember, a bargain is an attempt to close the negotiation and too early a strike for the deal may cause resentment. You may have not allowed the other side to put their case so as to give you the chance to consider it fully. Hence, the timing of the bargaining exchange is relevant.

Observation of body language in bargaining confirms the impression that people pay closer attention to the closing exchanges than they do in the opening and middle phases. This is understandable; the parties are closer to a decision than they were earlier, and this applies whether the final outcome is expected to be favourable or unfavourable. You sit up and forward, leaning onto the table, and you make determined eye contact (and sometimes with dilated pupils, such is your excitement). You listen attentively to details of how much of what you want is specifically on offer or for details of how much of a gap remains between their offer and your expectations.

Sure you could question the details, and I recommend that you do so for the usual reasons of clarification, but instant counter-bargains are irresistible, if the gap is close or some speedy reorganisation of the conditions or the offer suggests itself. In my experience, the impact of near-instant counter-bargains, compared with instant counter-proposals, is quite different. The former usually elicit near-instant counter-counter-bargains, while the latter usually result in slumps in the body language and a marked increase in tension.

Of course, sometimes attempts to modify a bargain more favourably to yourself will result in a slump in their body language and perhaps a slow expulsion of breath and a resigned open spread of their palms. They may be acting, or they may be at the end of the road – it depends on context and the seriousness of degree to which your bargain falls short of their requirements. (You too may be acting!)

What happens next is unpredictable at this distance from your negotiations. Broadly, you either go back into debates on each other's requirements and constraints, before returning to an amended bargain or a restatement of the previous one, or you tread water and slide towards a termination of the negotiations short of a deal.

Easy to deadlock

In negotiating there are many opportunities for them to break down, but the reality is not so clear-cut as the theory. People negotiate through their behaviours and their behaviours need not be conducive to them continuing to interact long enough to conclude a bargain.

All the traps of argument, talking past each other, mis-stating proposals, refusing to address (let alone 'consider') the other's interests, failed ploys and narrow vision are potentially present in the bargaining phase. People do not enter separate behavioural boxes labelled 'proposing' or 'bargaining' and, ratchet like, move only forwards and never backwards.

Activity 14.5

It is important for your learning activities that you pay close attention to the bargaining sequence in a current negotiation. Observe how a bargaining exchange can produce euphoria as you realise a deal is imminent, and also how a depressive mood quickly sets in as the deal appears to slip away.

Disengage mentally from the dispute and try to observe dispassionately how people react to either of these moods. Mutual euphoria usually produces co-operative gestures; mutual depression usually produces the opposite, with frustrated threats and blaming behaviours.

When the other side makes a bargaining statement, which, remember, is their firm proposal to settle, they are not immune to provocative interpretations of what they intend. They still cannot see inside each other's heads! It could be a question of timing (they tried to close the deal too soon) or of content (they ignored something important to the other side) or of manner (they sounded too pushy). Negotiations, therefore, are as likely to break down at any one time as another.

Moreover, as negotiations take time to process, events outside the deal could change the intentions of those inside. Consider, for example, long negotiations to end a strike in which a momentum among employees for a return to work builds up outside the talks; or in peace negotiations, when a sudden shift occurs in one side's fortunes on the battlefield. The disposition to settle on the existing terms is likely to change if the parties perceive differential advantages in slowing the progress that would otherwise be made.

Changing fortunes change commercial negotiations too. Announcements of a new technology could wipe out the price credibility of a proposed product and undermine the negotiating stances of the parties. A likely change in government is bound to undermine the perceived longevity of a Minister's policies if he loses office before the deal is struck. Similarly, divorce lawyers have been known to drag out negotiations on alimony if one of the parties wins a lottery (or gains a surprise inheritance), or to conclude them quickly if the win is not yet public (and estranged spouses also have been known to reassess their intentions in these circumstances).

Activity 14.6

Can you recollect a negotiated outcome that within a short time proved to be based on the wrong reading of the situation? Did the political, marketing or economic environment, or a technology change, make the deal redundant, uneconomic or misguided in some way?

It is not all doom and gloom by any means. The fragility of success is an element at any time, but particularly acute as time drags on. People sometimes simply change their minds, and not always for a good reason (such as the appearance of a better option from somebody else).

➡ BARGAINING TO A CLOSE

Bargaining is a time when you want to bring everybody to a decision. Anne Douglas, an early pioneer of research into bargaining behaviour, called this the 'decision crisis'.

This 'crisis' could work out with relative ease, because the amending counter-bargains have improved the acceptability of the deal, or they have at least not worsened it. But suppose you must settle at or very near where you stand with the current offered bargain. For you, it feels like 'now or never'. The plainest way to close the negotiation is for both of you to accept the bargain as it stands. Saying 'Yes' to a bargain always closes the negotiation.

In the absence of a 'Yes', I recommend the following bargaining behaviours. They are set out in ascending order of difficulty of applying them. The third behaviour listed is particulalry risky as it could shut the door on a settlement. You are back on the tightrope.

- The 'summary bargain' is self-explanatory. Summarise the bargain, emphasising, perhaps, how much you both have put into the proposed deal and the sacrifices both sides have made to get this far. If it genuinely is perceived as the best deal both can get, then agreement should follow.

- The 'small traded-movement bargain' is a reactive bargain to some small difficulty contained in the current proposal. I emphasise 'small' because if it is a large difficulty and it provokes movement, clearly the bargaining is not over. But sometimes a small difficulty is identified as the only barrier to securing an agreement. This is a matter of judgement, for opening up detailed issues for amendment could send all the wrong signals. To obviate a run of 'small' amendments, you must insist on them being traded. That always slows down the appetite for raising issues for amendment because they never know what you will come up with for counter-amendment. Assuming the amendment is identified and traded, you summarise the deal as above.

- The 'adjournment' bargain summarises the deal and suggests an adjournment for both parties to consider their options. As with all proposals for an adjournment, set a date and time for reconvening to process the decision. Parties taking the time to reflect on the pluses and minuses sometimes decide that the former outweigh the latter and decide to settle. The risk is that, in the intervening time, new options are discovered or one party realises that the minuses outweigh the pluses.

Pressure in the adjournment is increased by presenting it as a forced decision with a deadline for acceptance or its withdrawal, followed by the termination of the relationship. Red behaviours, such as statements to 'take it or leave it' or 'accept it or else' usually presage a termination!

Activity 14.7

How have your recent negotiations ended? Did you come to a crunch in some way? If so, which side pushed the button to force the decision? Did the parties use some version of the bargaining closes listed above? What triggered the final deal?

➡ RECORDING WHAT WAS AGREED

Whatever the behaviours prior to the decision, once a decision is made to accept the bargain it is advisable for you to record that acceptance in an acceptable form and for both sides to agree by detailed summary to what they believe they have agreed. This cannot be emphasised too strongly, as later disagreements over what was agreed leads only to a souring of relationships and, sometimes, recriminations and charges of 'bad faith'.

The euphoria of the close to a negotiation is dangerous when it induces laxness in your recording the detail of what you agreed. While your colleagues pop the champagne, do not delegate but ensconce yourself with the other side's people, going over everything together to create a document worthy of signature by both parties. Whatever the temptation, I urge you to ignore waiting planes and the natural *bonhomie* after the handshakes and spend your time agreeing what you agreed.

For your toolkit

T14.1 Make your bargaining statements specific in the condition and the offer.

T14.2 Always (no exceptions) state the bargains in the 'if–then' format.

T14.3 After stating your specific bargain, shut up!

T14.4 You may instantly counter-bargain, changing the specific condition, or the specific offer, or both.

T14.5 In responding to a bargain, question the terms for understanding.

T14.6 Saying 'Yes' to a bargain closes the negotiation.

T14.7 To complete the 'decision crisis', summarise the terms of the bargain.

T14.8 To secure agreement, consider a small traded movement on a small detail.

T14.9 To extend the opportunity for a decision, summarise the terms and suggest an adjournment for mutual consideration, stating precise times and venue for reconvening.

T14.10 On agreement, record what has been agreed in an acceptable form and require each party to sign the agreed record before the meeting adjourns.

Chapter 15
Competitive and co-operative bargaining strategies

➡ INPUTS AND OUTPUTS

You do not negotiate in a vacuum. Businesses exist in the environment, not in the abstract. That environment defines the nature of the relationship between the negotiating parties, be they externally related (as with suppliers and customers) or internally related (as within the functions of the organisation).

Business organisations traditionally buy their inputs from external suppliers, to which they add value through processing and/or through changing the location of the inputs, and they sell their outputs to external customers. For instance, a newspaper business buys inputs such as newsprint, ink, machines, editorial copy, electricity, and so on, and processes these to produce its outputs, the newspaper. It sells its newspapers to customers through wholesale and retail distribution chains. Its customers purchase the newspaper for its information or entertainment content.

Business organisations can also be seen as chains of internal suppliers and internal customers. Each function in the chain receives inputs from internal sources and processes the inputs to move them to the next function in the chain. For example, a machine-room function receives inputs from the stores function (its internal supplier – they both work for the same organisation) and processes them (shaping, drilling, planing, polishing, painting, etc.,) and then passes the finished output to an internal customer, the assembly function, which ultimately, via the despatch function, delivers the output to the organisation's external customers.

It does not matter whether you work in a manufacturing or a servicing function, the essence of the process is a transaction along similar lines: input–process–output. But how the parties perceive their environments – external and internal – moulds how they conduct their relationships. Not the least aspect of their relationship is that of how they negotiate and bargain with each other.

Activity 15.1

Construct a process chain for your business, showing the external suppliers and external customers on either side of a box marked 'added-value process' (that is, what your business does to whatever it processes).

Now expand the box marked 'added-value process' to construct at least one process chain for your internal suppliers and customers for your function (you probably have many different chains passing through your function).

Label the identities of your external/internal suppliers and your external/internal customers. Who are they? How do you relate to them? What is the nature of your negotiating relationships with them?

➡ COMPETITIVE BARGAINING

There are two models for bargaining, one of which is purely competitive. This red-style model affects attitudes and behaviour and is deeply entrenched in business environments. You have probably come across it in the buying function – or perhaps you are an exponent of it as a business buyer!

Activity 15.2

Are you in, or have you had contact with, a company's buying function? How would you describe the negotiating behaviours of the buyers – red or blue?

Why do you think buyers traditionally appear to behave in a red manner? Is it their personality or a necessary aspect of their function's culture?

How would you compare the buyers' behaviours that you work for, or with, to the behaviours of people working in sales functions? Are they more red or more blue than buyers?

Why do you think there is a difference in their general behaviours? Is it something in their personalities or something to do with their respective functions?

The traditional measure of the success of a firm's buying function is in its containment of the costs of purchase. In short: buy cheaply! The methods used to buy cheaply – defined as 'any price lower than a seller's best price' – are predictable. First, for every item of supply, find several suppliers willing to compete for a share in the quantities required by the company. Secondly, no matter how good a single supplier's price, do not award the total supply to that one supplier but keep some other suppliers under contract to supply the remainder, even if it means paying higher prices for their identical products. Thirdly, use the relationship with other suppliers to exert competitive pressure on all suppliers. Finally, maintain some capacity for making the product in house if possible.

Procurement managers who can report actual purchasing costs for inputs below the budgeted costs are rewarded; those who report actual purchasing costs above the budgeted costs are not. In the extreme, a record for variations in supply prices above budgeted costs is a one-way ticket to termination. Hence, procurement managers strive to drive the variation down below their budgets. Their delegates get the message and behave accordingly. This is the 'variance' model of procurement.

Activity 15.3

How would you think that buyers, in a culture that encourages them to procure supplies below the budgeted amounts allocated to their acquisition, will behave when they interview potential sellers?

Buyers as negotiators behave in a red manner, use red ploys, and have red attitudes. They believe that sellers pad their prices and are not satisfied until they find and strip away the padding. Sellers who anticipate this behaviour, pad their prices to have something to strip away. A vicious circle ensues in which each side lives the nightmare it believes the other side concocts for it.

Red bargaining strategies

There are not many blue buyers in business, or more correctly, there are not many old blue buyers in business. They get weeded out long before they get promoted. Red buyers are the norm in those businesses – the majority? – who conform to the variance model of procurement: 'Whatever you do as a buyer, make sure that your spend line is always below your budget line.' Included in the 'whatever else you do' sentiment, is an admonition in favour of quality, or fitness for purpose; but in the struggle between price and budget, the pressure is taken by quality. Suppliers with little profit in their prices are bound to cut corners.

Consider the consequence of many years of applying the variance model to the procurement function in a manufacturing business I once researched. They made high-technology products (missiles, or, as their sales manager called them 'hittiles' because 'we don't ship anything likely to miss!') and bought in a considerable number of specialised components, which they assembled under very strict production conditions ('Clean 100' rooms, etc.). Some of these components had a low unit cost, mainly brought about by having eight or more suppliers engaged in stiff competition to 'win' purchase orders. Every negotiation was intensely red in behaviour and outcome. The suppliers were pushed, cajoled and intimidated into constant price cuts by threats of delisting as suppliers and of their purchase quantities being transferred to their more compliant competitors.

One such component was a simple spring washer. Procurement had got the cost down to 25 pence a washer. The variance looked good; congratulations all round. The washer also snapped easily. When it did, it had to be replaced. That imposed 'rework' costs on the production function. Sometimes these costs could be very high, as when the missile showed malfunctions after post-delivery calibration testing. Returning the defective missile to the plant, stripping it down, replacing the defective parts, deGaussing the reassembled missile, recalibrating it and returning it to the customer was very expensive – and a lot more than the cost of the replacement washers.

In other words, the cost of purchase – by which the purchasing function is judged – is insufficient to capture the full cost of supply, by which a business is judged.

Activity 15.4

What does it cost in your line of work to redo jobs you have completed, be it a product, a report, a service or even an invoice returned for amendment?

What is the incidence of rework in your function? Have you any idea of its annual (monthly) cost?

The savings in procurement were being wiped out by the on-costs in production. When this was noticed by the top management (they knew their key ratios!), it was not long before they re-examined the assumptions behind their procurement culture and found them wanting. The traditional variance model was gradually replaced by a new bargaining strategy. The number of suppliers for all components was reconsidered. They embarked on a programme of halving the number of suppliers within a procurement cycle and then reducing them again to one or two per component.

They selected suppliers who would *collaborate* with them in reducing the total cost of supply (which included eliminating reworking costs from poor quality) within an agreed profit level for themselves and with the security of large annual or biannual purchase orders. The last I heard was that the unit cost of the washers had risen to 45 pence but the engineering rework linked to snapped washers had been virtually eliminated.

Activity 15.5

How many suppliers per component do you buy from in your function?

Take a recent major purchase, and go over how your department selected the supplier. Was it one from several? By tender? By

repurchase from the previous supplier? How would you describe
your function's bargaining behaviour?

Some smart procurement experts think they can lick the
'snapping washer' type of problem with an even redder buying
strategy that is not so crude in its manner but is more effective. I
refer to the practice of 'silent competition' by inference and not by
openly aggressive behaviour, such as is more commonly exhibited.

In this red buying strategy, the procurement function draws up a
performance specification to estabish the quality standard that
they expect and will pay for. Experience suggests that the more
detailed the spec, the more difficult it is to monitor and ensure
quality, and so the simpler the product the easier it is to apply a
quality spec. However, exponents of this strategy are seldom
modest about its alleged advantages (cockiness, I find, goes with a
red buyer's territory!) and insist that they can achieve the expected
quality standards with as detailed a spec as is necessary. If the
existing spec is not tight enough, then they increase the spec.

Next, the red buyer issues the spec and invites a number of
potential suppliers to submit their proposals by a given date. In
due course, those suppliers wishing to make bids do so. The red
buyer studies the bids but otherwise does nothing. After a time,
most bidders call the buyer to enquire about the progress of their
bids. The red buyer springs the first stage of the bargaining trap.
She tells each caller that their bid has been received but they are
above the lowest bid price. She resolutely refuses to indicate what
that lower bid price might be or which other companies have
made bids. All she tells them is that if they want to rebid they
should do so.

Activity 15.6

How do you think suppliers react to the situation just described?
Do they bid or not bid?
  What would you do?

It doesn't matter really how many rebid as long as at least one of
them does so. According to red strategists, most of the bidders
rebid. By convention, a rebid is a lower price bid than the original

bid. The strategy can be varied slightly, by requiring rebidders to improve their bids with elements from the offers to supply from other bidders.

After a time, the rebidders will make enquiries about the fate of their rebids and once again the buyer tells each caller that their bid has been received but they are still above the lowest bid price. As before she resolutely refuses to indicate what that lower bid price might be or which other companies have made bids. All she tells them (again) is that if they want to rebid they should do so.

How long can this go on for? For as long as at least one of the sellers rebids! Remember, the seller does not know against whom he is bidding, nor what price he has to beat to win the business. Indeed, he does not know if there is anybody else bidding nor whether he is the lowest bidder. He could be the only bidder and he could be bidding against himself. The buyer is very much in the driving seat – assuming sellers are gullible enough to play the game – and she can keep the game going for as long as she wants. She has no responsibility for the price the seller offers, but she knows that every rebid price is likely to be lower than the previous one.

All the competitive pressure works on the seller through the seller's perceptions of what his competitors are doing – even though every competitor may have dropped out and he is the only one left playing. It does not require heavy red behavioural pressure from the buyer – she remains aloof and full of sympathetic sweetness – because it is the seller's imagination that provides all the pressure needed.

➡ BARGAINING LEVERAGE MODELS

Competition theorists, such as Michael Porter at Harvard, held sway over much of industrial strategy by articulating a bargaining model that corresponds to the way many firms see their role in the markets they trade in.

Porter identifies five competitive pressures on the firm. These are:

1. firms within the same business sector (particularly your immediate rivals, who supply similar products)
2. new technologies that could substantially change the technological

basis of your business sector (e.g. you are in CD-ROMs and
suddenly an interactive digital product appears)

3. new entrants joining your business sector (e.g. mutual building
societies becoming banks)

4. the bargaining power of your customers

5. the bargaining power of your suppliers

It is the bargaining power of your customers and suppliers that I
am concerned with. This is a red competitive model. It reflects the
mores of its times (the mid-1980s in the USA). It has some useful
lessons for you in bargaining strategy.

Activity 15.7

How would you rate your business against Porter's five competitive
pressures?

This activity basically requires you to identify your competitors
within your business sector; to assess the technological threats on
(or over) the horizon; to identify if there are any potential new
entrants lurking near your business sector; to assess the bargaining
leverage of your suppliers over your firm (and vice versa); and to
assess the bargaining leverage of your firm over your customers (or
vice versa).

Porter's point, and one endorsed by many of the executives
exposed to his model, is that the notion of bargaining leverage
from suppliers and customers conforms to experience.

If you have suppliers who trade in a scarce resource essential to
your business, they are likely to be able to extract high unit prices
and to impose other – perhaps onerous – conditions on you. This is
what is meant by a supplier's bargaining leverage. For example, in
the wholesale distribution of newspapers, periodicals and journals
in Scotland, one wholesaler, for historical and geographical
reasons, had a virtual monopoly. This meant that in its dealings
with retail newsagents it could limit discounts even to fairly large
retail chains and strictly limit them to the thousands of independ-
ents. Effectively, it controlled the profit margins of the retailers on
these commodities.

At the other end of the spectrum, if there are many suppliers of a product that is not unique and not a major element in your business – pencils, say – it is unlikely that they can exert significant bargaining leverage over you, nor perhaps you over them. You can buy pencils anywhere, almost, and they can sell pencils anywhere. The loss or gain of your small-quantity order will neither trouble nor enthuse them.

Similarly, with customers. A high-value sale of product to a few customers allows these customers to exert bargaining leverage. For example, in the undersea telecommunications cable business there are about five suppliers in the world, each of which has the technology and the industrial capacity to supply many thousands of miles of cable required to fulfil a single order. However, there are only about two or three such large orders per year. Not winning one of these orders means gross excess capacity for that year in the supplier companies affected by the order drought. This gives the telecom companies bargaining leverage over the suppliers.

Activity 15.8

On the basis of the foregoing information in this section, can you identify the causes of red behaviour from the possession or absence of bargaining leverage?

In dynamic economies, no situation remains frozen for long. Bargaining leverage relationships change. Factors stimulating such change are as follows:

- New entrants can upset cosy monopolies or steady-state oligopolies with new pricing and marketing structures. This was the intention behind the public sector privatisations, although the outcome has been of mixed success in performance (though good for the public treasury).

- New technologies can disrupt an entire business sector and shift the bargaining advantages of suppliers and customers. This has certainly happened in computing and threatens to happen in digital television.

- Changes within the organisations of competing rivals can shake a sector every bit as fundamentally as new entrants and new technologies. This is still happening in financial services, although in this sector it is really a combination of organisational change *and* new technology.

- Dormant firms under new management can reshape a sector out of recognition. An example of this phenomenon is found in retail shopping in the rivalry between Tesco and Sainsbury in out-of-town shopping, and perhaps in the mergers of international accountancy firms and their effects on audit practice.

Flaws in bargaining leverage strategies

Can you alter the business environment to make it more favourable for bargaining? The red bargainers clearly think so, although they choose to do so by methods not necessarily in their best interests (think of the snapping washers).

I am thinking of a different approach and one that is gaining increasing recognition as an alternative bargaining strategy. It is not for every business sector, nor for every business in a sector. But it is worthy of your consideration, whatever your business.

Re-examine the implications of seeking bargaining leverage over your suppliers and customers. In what way are you competing with your suppliers? In the bargaining leverage model the answer is 'obvious': lowering the costs of purchase goes straight to the bottom line. Save a pound on a purchase and you add a pound to your profits – what could be clearer? What business would not be happy doing that? And what business would want to add a pound to its purchases? (Of course, this ignores the cost of supply.)

OK, for the moment, I will put your answer to one side and ask, 'In what way are you competing with your customers?' The bargaining leverage model also classes the answer among the 'obvious': raising the price at which you sell your goods adds to total revenue and, provided that your revenue is profitable, that net profit goes to the bottom line. Add a pound to revenue and you add some portion of that pound to profit. What could be clearer? What business would not be happy doing that? And what business would want to reduce a pound from its revenue?

These answers suggest that you see your relationships with your suppliers and customers in zero-sum terms. Take a pound of your payments to suppliers and it adds a pound to your profit; add a pound to your sales revenue and it adds some proportion of itself (because it is net of the cost of sales and overheads) to your profit.

Activity 15.9

On the basis of the differential effect on profits, can you see why the buying function is the more popular function for deploying red behaviour?

Why are sellers less red than buyers?

Can you also see why the selling function attracts more resources in sales support than the buying function receives in buying support?

Why are sellers usually paid more than buyers, even though red success in buying adds more to profit than sales?

But take a wider view of your business in a competitive market. With whom are you *really* in competition? Yes, your rivals in other firms! If market sector volumes are stable, then a growth in your sales is at the expense of the sales of your rivals. Every one of your customers who buys from you is not buying from your rivals; your rivals' customers are not buying from you. You are in a zero-sum relationship with your competitors. So why are you competing with your customers? Surely, you compete with the competitors who can supply your customers?

Now look at your suppliers. They supply you and your competitors (assuming you have similar inputs). Why are you competing with your suppliers? Surely, you compete with your competitors, who also buy their inputs from your suppliers. Special attention given to your rivals' interests by your suppliers reduces the attention they can give to *your* interests, and vice versa.

Bargaining leverage strategies work *against* your competitive interests because they focus on the wrong targets. They focus on your suppliers and your customers instead of on your rivals. With your suppliers you have compatible interests; with your competitors you have none. With your customers you have compatible interests; with your competitors you have none. Is this not a flaw in a strategy of bargaining leverage, even before we factor in consideration of the relatively short time span in which a bargaining advantage might operate?

➡ CO-OPETITION

An alternative model for bargaining behaviour has recently been advanced. It brings together the words 'co-operation' and 'competition' to form 'co-opetition'. The idea is less of a mouthful than the name for it.

At its root, a co-opetition strategy recognises that you are not in a state of all-out conflict with everybody – suppliers, customers and competitors. (What a red mindset is implied in that stance!) Co-opetition distinguishes between those with whom you have compatible interests and those with whom you have competing interests.

Prime facie, your suppliers are among those with whom you have compatible interests. You depend upon them when you add value to their products by incorporating them in yours. If you add their inputs to form your output and they fail to meet the standard, it is your product that is compromised in your customer's opinion. This is very visible in products that include many components imported into them from many suppliers, but it is no less true for products (including services) that use bought-in inputs to a much smaller extent, or use inputs invisible to the customer.

Motor vehicles, for example, take inputs from parts manufacturers. If these fail in service, the maker of the vehicle, rather than the part, suffers the indignation of the affected driver and perhaps loses reputation among other drivers and from that sales of branded vehicles. It is in the interests of the vehicle manufacturer to forge close links with its suppliers of parts to ensure that the best production techniques, materials and design are incorporated into what they supply. These may mean sharing information, research and development, and design costs so as to improve constantly the inputs – and thus the outputs that incorporate the inputs.

In the case of the supply of a service, where the supplier's inputs are not so visible, the same compatibility of interests may exist. A service dependent on information is only as good as the quantity of the information, its timely delivery, and its quality. It is not much use having an e-mail address if the server keeps going off-line; a restaurant with a faulty credit-card machine is going to detract from its food quality if the customers cannot pay without fuss; and a comedian who retells jokes supplied by a writing service is not going to raise many laughs if the audience considers the jokes to be in poor taste.

This strategy of co-opetition requires a different negotiating stance from that required by a strategy of searching for bargaining leverage. For a start, the broad stance must be one of 'partnership' and not rivalry.

Activity 15.10

Make a first cut at a co-opetition audit of your business. List your suppliers and check how many supply the same products. What do your aggregate purchases for each item sum to, and would this sum be worth seeking a co-opetition relationship to supply? In what ways would you prefer to see the product improved? Have you got any ideas about how they could improve their services?

Do the same for your major customers. How could you improve what you supply to them and how could they help you do that?

Even the prospect of an exclusive relationship with a supplier or customer could be sufficient to create interest in co-opetition. Would you like exclusive relationships with your customer (i.e., they buy only from you)?

For your toolkit

T15.1 Buying cheap and selling dear may not be in your best long-term interests.

T15.2 When invited to bid for business, make clear that you will only bid once.

T15.3 Bargaining leverage models are not in your long-term interests.

T15.4 Do not try to compete with your suppliers or your customers. Compete only with your competitors.

T15.5 Partners are not rivals.

T15.6 Undertake co-opetition audits of your suppliers and customers and negotiate co-opetition relationships.

Chapter 16
Alongside negotiation

➡ EXPLICIT AND IMPLICIT BARGAINS

Negotiation skills address a specific set of problems, usually some version of how to get what you want through trade. Other people control the resources that you need to do your job. In so far as the acquisition of these resources is subject to negotiation, the tools developed in the previous chapters will assist you in your quest for them. But what of those resources that are not normally subject to negotiation? How do you acquire them peacefully?

It is appropriate to introduce you to a range of techniques that are closely associated with negotiation but not identical either in their design or application. I refer here to a subject broadly known as 'influencing'. Necessarily, my coverage of influencing is brief, selective and focused.

If asked the difference between negotiation and influencing, I reply that in negotiation the bargain is 'explicit', while in influencing the 'bargain' is 'implicit'. Recall that the negotiated bargain is specific in both the condition and the offer and, once agreed, it closes the negotiation process. The next step after agreement is to implement the negotiated decisions. Each party has pledged to deliver what they have agreed and to implement their side of the bargain. Each party, therefore, is aware of what they have agreed and explicitly volunteers to meet their commitments.

In commercial practice, non-compliance with the agreements (contracts) that people make is penalised, and aggrieved parties seek compensatory remedies in the courts for the non-performance of contractual obligations. Contracts, despite the numerous breaches of them, are worth a lot more than the paper they are written on, and many lawyers make a great deal of money from aggrieved parties who prosecute their disputes.

➡ WHAT IS INFLUENCING?

With influencing we enter a completely different world. There are no legally binding contracts; there are no explicit performance criteria; disputes, of which there are many, seldom if ever get to a courtroom; and nobody but the parties involved knows what was implied by their influencing behaviour. Indeed, in many cases the parties could reasonably deny that they were influenced, or that they influenced, each other. What a strange world!

But you have not worked long as a manager if you are unaware of the role of influencing all around your job function. At first, your awareness may be slight, a mere rumour, or a feeling that things are not quite as they seem. Given time, you soon become aware that the way things get done around you does not correspond neatly to the formal job definitions of the people with whom you interact. How you react marks you out within your organisation and to a large extent determines your progress within it.

Influencing is about pursuing strategies, usually 'upwards' or 'sideways' within an organisation, to achieve predetermined ends that are important to you. I confine 'influencing' to upwards or sideways behaviour because influencing downwards is usually about leadership – for which subject there is a large and growing literature ('leadership' is probably the most intensely researched subject in management studies).

The tools of influencing are many and varied. I shall select from them two that are closely related to negotiating.

Reciprocation

I have already introduced the behaviour of reciprocation, the history of which is as long as that of the history of exchange behaviour. Reciprocation is distinguished from explicit bargaining, which is simultaneous, conditional and contingent by being sequential, unconditional and non-contingent.

Normally, sequential, unconditional and non-contingent behaviours would be a heavy burden to overcome in order to work. But, the mores of reciprocation are extremely strong, widely practised and well understood, particularly when they are breached. Reciprication is a universally practised behaviour across the entire human species.

Activity 16.1

Think of some recent favour or 'good turn' you did for somebody else. Ignore your motives in doing it. Suppose, now, that an opportunity arises in which you would greatly benefit – and for which you would be mightily pleased – if they returned a favour of equal or lesser magnitude for you. Suppose also that they do not oblige, though it is well within their gift to do so. How would you feel about them and their act of not reciprocating the favour?

Overwhelmingly, the majority (all?) of people who undertake Activity 16.1 express some degree of dissatisfaction, if not disgust, at a person who does not reciprocate a favour.

Scratch the surface of a personal antagonism between two people and you will often find an instance, or repeated instances, of non-reciprocation lurking close to the top. Certainly, in my counselling experience of disputes between people, the most severe intra-familial disputes are always about a 'betrayal of trust' (usually sexual) or an act of non-reciprocation (even of a relatively trivial nature). Of the two causes of these disputes, acts of non-reciprocation seems to be the last to be forgiven!

Activity 16.2

Go back as far as you like in your life story – to primary school or to last week – and recall why you fell out with somebody about whom you had previously felt warm? Was it an act of non-reciprocation that triggered the switch in your feelings?

Evolutionary psychologists make much of this strange phenomenon. You and I only need to recognise its power to mould the behaviour of others in today's world. And so, if you want to influence people you had better tune into other people's reciprocation sensitivities.

Activity 16.3

Complete the sentence: 'One good turn deserves ... .'

I have never met anybody who cannot complete that sentence correctly. And studying the anthropological records in many non-English-speaking societies, I have noted the frequency with which similar sentiments are expressed as a cause of the interpersonal disputes in them. That should tell you something about the universality of the expectation of reciprocation.

Let me dispose of an ethical objection that sometimes surfaces at this point. Some people argue that you should do good turns because good turns are good to do, and you should not do them in the expectation of a returned good turn at some point in the future. This is often accompanied by virulent assertions that they do good turns without the slightest wish to have them reciprocated. Indeed, they take it as insulting that I appear to be saying that they do!

Let me be clear. Such intentions are not in question here. Of course, some people do good turns without thought of recompense, for few of us calculate the future so finely. But that is not what reciprocation is about. Of necessity, it does not look forward. The problem arises not while the good turn is being done but after it is done at some time in the future. When the good turn is firmly in the past, and an opportunity to return a favour is evaded (for whatever reason) in the future, your reciprocation code switches on. The reciprocation ledger looks backwards, not forwards. It is at that point that the negative reaction sets in and not before. You may have had the disinterested intentions of a saint, but your intentions will be sorely tested when you feel let down by someone whom you have helped previously and whose help you need with something that is important to you.

For influencing, then, it is recommended that you do people good turns and rely on their felt obligations to return the good

turns when it is important for you that they do. In the main –
there are always defectors – people reciprocate.

To complete the message, be wary of the opposite of good turns.

Activity 16.4

Complete the sentence: 'One bad turn deserves ... .'

I am sure you got that one too! You can avoid negative influence
working against your interests by making sure that you do not
carelessly do people bad turns. They remember your bad turns with
an even greater ferocity than they remember your non-reciprocation of their good turns. 'Hell hath no fury ... ,' etc. when it comes
to reciprocating bad turns.

Currencies of exchange

In influencing, money is not the currency of exchange (I am
excluding here the corrupt buying of influence, which is truly
unethical). People trade in many 'currencies', and if you wish to
influence them you must identify the currencies they exchange
and, if your influence goal is important enough to you, you must
then transact with them in those currencies.

An influencing currency is anything, tangible or intangible, that
the other person regards as important for them. They do not
necessarily articulate or advertise the influencing currencies that
they trade in, and you will have to observe what it is that they
regard as important.

Activity 16.5

Think of somebody you need to influence in your job function. Try
to identify the kinds of things they like to experience. For example,
do they like to feel important? Do they like to get their picture in
the company newsletter? Do they like praise or the respect of their
peers?

What, in your view makes them tick, and purr like a contented
cat? Those things are indicators of the currencies they trade in.

Influencing currencies are numerous, personal and tradable, provided that you can identify them and you have the resources (including the inclination) to supply them. For instance, a manager who likes 'visibility' will be put out if you deliberately (or inadvertently) deny her the visibility she craves (and guess which motive she will ascribe to your behaviour!). Therefore, the influencer asks: 'Can I help her become more visible?' Alternatively, a manager who is more comfortable with 'vision' (where the business is going) than with 'detail' (how it will get there) is not comfortable with people who decry his vision and lumber him with detail, especially if the detail is perceived as negative obstacles created to compromise the vision.

Conversely, a manager with an attention to detail is soon put off by too much 'vision' and not enough practical detail. Politicians, concerned with the governance of their country (which involves detail), lose patience with politicians with too little to do, and who speak in visions and have no sense of detail. Make sure you get it right when dealing with them as either visionaries or detail managers.

Activity 16.6

What currencies do you prefer to trade in? In other words, what do you like people to do for you?

➡ THE OBJECTIVES OF INFLUENCING

The influencer does good turns and trades in currencies for a purpose. They want something to be done for them. The nature of influencing requires that they expend considerable time inducing the habit of mutual reciprocation of many small favours, as they build relationships with those around them. And this is better than building a bank of favours for eventual reciprocation in one go.

Activity 16.7

What do you want to influence others to do for you at work? Is it

promotion, or new responsibilities, or more resources for your
function, or whatever?

Your influencing objectives are as wide an agenda as your job
function allows. Only you can decide what these are to be, and
only you can assess how important the objectives are for you and
to what extent you will dedicate your influencing activities to
secure them.

The targets of your influencing strategy are the people who have
the power to deliver your objectives. These will chiefly be more
senior than you or on a par with you in other job functions, but as
you never know who will leap up the management tree to
positions above you, you cannot neglect including as targets
people currently junior to you in the organisation.

When you begin an influencing strategy you may have nothing
specific in mind other than a vague notion that you need more
than the merits of your case or position to achieve what you want.
You may also have no particular targets in mind. This leads to the
conclusion that your influencing behaviour is not going to be
focused on particular individuals until you have identified what
you want and who is in a position to deliver it.

From this conclusion, it follows that as you do not know who is
or will be in a position to help you at some indeterminate date in
the future, you are going to have to be indiscriminate in your
influencing behaviour. That is not a bad thing because it means
that everybody you interact with will be treated no differently.
They will all benefit from your good turns and the resulting
potential currency trades.

To do otherwise, especially with senior managers, traps you into
the familiar and disreputable acts of 'brown-nosing', as our
American cousins somewhat inelegantly put it. Being selective in
your behaviour is soon spotted by those excluded from it, and you
will earn the reputation you deserve. The excluded then become
antagonists and possible sources of counter-influence, and some of
the included, who become aware of your partiality, become too
embarrassed to help you.

There is no sensible way round this, and from a behavioural
point of view that is to your benefit and to the benefit of those
around you. Even if driven by the most cynical of motives, the

influencer behaves in the most positive of ways towards *everybody*. You behave as a 'nicer' person and, to all intents and purposes, you *are* a 'nicer' person, and over a long-enough period, and with practice, you genuinely become a nicer person.

➡ ON SELECTION BY MERIT

Activity 16.8

To what extent do you consider ideas, the people selected for promotion, the projects selected for support, and the distribution of resources, are decided on their merits in your organisation?

Think of one of these categories. Can you think of any competing ideas, people, projects or use of resources, that also had merit but did not win enough support? Why didn't they win support?

Can you think of any ideas, people, projects or use of resources that were selected in the past that did not stand the test of time? How did they get selected?

Belief in management by merit is seldom seriously argued by experienced managers. They soon realise, by observation and awareness of their own disappointments, that something more than merit is required to win selection in a management hierarchy, even a flat one!

Simply sending in your report and your recommendations to a competitive selection meeting and relying on them to come to the same decision as you seek is either extremely arrogant or courageous. In management it is also somewhat naïve. In the absence of authority to get your way, you will probably have to lobby, and the best base to lobby from is one built on an influencing strategy targeted to at least one person at the meeting – preferably more than one.

I make the necessary assumption, for this exercise, that your proposal has merit at least comparable to the other competing proposals. Influencing, like selling, is not a strategy for supplying duff products. Indeed, using influence to pass off a duff proposal as one with merit is extremely foolhardy and a fast way to *lose* influence with those you deceive into backing your proposal.

Making people look bad by backing you is to trade in a depreciating currency.

At the primary level, your influencing strategy makes you known to those around and above you. They have seen or heard you at work and, because you supply currencies they trade in, they are at least neutral towards you and, hopefully, some have positive feelings for you. When, in the past, you interacted directly with members of the selection meeting, you did them good not bad turns and you were sensitive to their influencing currencies. So, when it was appropriate to supply their currencies, you did so. This will count in the selection meeting, if only because your rivals (it is assumed here) did not invest in a conscious influencing strategy, or they were too selective, or their influencing was conducted over too short a time period. It is no good trying to influence close to a crucial meeting because your new-found enthusiasm for the members will be transparent. You come across like a politician who visits constituents only during election time and you attract commensurate cynicism.

How do I know this will happen or that your rival's campaigns will be ineffective? Mainly from observing how bad most people are at influencing. They are much worse at the implicit bargain (influencing) than they are at the explicit bargain (negotiating), and mostly they are not too good at the latter.

Large dividends are earned from developing influencing strategies in your organisation. I have only introduced two elements of such a strategy, mainly to provide a 'taster' for a longer investigation by yourself of influencing. Influencing skills in combination with negotiation skills provide a formidable skill set for managers who want to get up, get going and get on with their careers. Nothing in the necessary skill sets for negotiating and influencing needs to be unethical or morally dubious. You do only what you are comfortable doing, commensurate with the importance to you of your objectives.

Social exchange is one of the most powerful of humanising behaviours created by our human heritage. Sharpening your skills in social exchange processes, including negotiation and influencing, is a positive contribution to social harmony. It surely beats relying on your other inherited behaviours of red (as in tooth and claw) and blue (as in supine submission).

And negotiation makes you human by neutralising the red and blue in you through the altogether more useful form of purple conditionality. *Ex bona fide negotiari.*

For your toolkit

T16.1 One good turn deserves another, but also one bad turn deserves another.

T16.2 Do good turns to others indiscriminately.

T16.3 Identify the influencing currencies of those around you and supply them, where possible, indiscriminately.

T16.4 Identify the targets of your influencing strategy and direct good turns and currency exchanges to them and to those around them.

Appendix
The Negotek® Competence Test

A short multiple-choice test follows for you to test your understanding of the main concepts presented in the text. Please choose the most appropriate answer from those provided.

1. **We should NEGOTIATE when:**

   a) it would be a sign of weakness to give in
   b) we need them more than they need us
   c) both parties can say 'No'
   d) when they need us more than we need them

2. **A negotiator's ENTRY PRICE is:**

   a) the price she prefers
   b) the price she must get
   c) the price she thinks the other negotiator will pay
   d) a credible starting point

3. **The SETTLEMENT RANGE is the range between the negotiators' overlapping:**

   a) exit prices
   b) entry and exit prices
   c) entry prices
   d) exit and entry prices

4. **BLUE BEHAVIOUR is characterised by:**

   a) being submissive and generous

- b) giving more than you take
  c) being assertive
  d) intending to make the other negotiator happy

5. **Negotiators PRIORITISE:**

   a) ranges
   b) entry and exit points
 - c) tradables
   d) negotiable issues

6. **A WANT is:**

   a) a subissue
 - b) a preferred outcome
   c) a range
   d) an unobtainable need

7. **In the DEBATE PHASE you should:**

   a) complete it as quickly as possible to avoid argument
 - b) discover the other negotiator's wants
 - c) ensure that the other negotiator understands your positions
   d) refrain from disclosing your wants

8. **An INTEREST is:**

   a) anything that is important to a negotiator
   b) something the negotiators have in common
 - c) a motive for preferring one outcome over another
   d) the negotiators' hidden agendas

9. **Negotiators SIGNAL to indicate:**

 - a) a willingness to move
   b) a desire for the listener to move
 - c) that a proposal is imminent
   d) a preference for conceding

10. **The most effective way to handle a DISAGREEMENT is to:**

    a) only point out where the other negotiator is factually wrong
    b) ask questions
    c) explain courteously the grounds for your disagreement
    d) summarise the case against the other negotiator's views

11. **PURPLE BEHAVIOUR is characterised by:**

    a) linking red and blue behaviour
    b) adding blue to red behaviour
    c) neutralising red behaviour with blue offers
    d) linking red conditions with blue offers

12. **In the PROPOSAL PHASE a negotiator should:**

    a) ask questions
    b) be non-specific in the CONDITION and specific in the OFFER
    c) be specific in the CONDITION and specific in the OFFER
    d) be specific in the CONDITION and non-specific in the OFFER

13. **A TRADABLE is:**

    a) anything you want to trade
    b) anything on the agenda
    c) anything over which the negotiators have discretion
    d) anything you prefer

14. **A BARGAIN is:**

    a) a specific CONDITION and a non-specific OFFER
    b) a specific CONDITION and a specific OFFER
    c) a non-specific CONDITION and a specific OFFER
    d) a good deal

15. **EFFECTIVE NEGOTIATORS:**

    a) always prepare before they negotiate
    b) bargain after they have proposed
    c) behave appropriately in each phase

d) always signal before they propose

16. RED BEHAVIOUR is characterised by:

   a) being aggressive and rude
—b) taking more than you give
   c) being submissive
   d) intending to humiliate the other negotiator

If you would like me to comment on your answers, or if you have any comments on the test, please send a stamped addressed envelope (or postal coupons) to: Dr Gavin Kennedy, 99 Caiyside, Edinburgh EH10 7HR, Scotland, UK. Please allow 28 days for a reply (I am sometimes away on an assignment). Or e-mail your responses to "Gavin Kennedy" ⟨gavin@neg1.demon.co.uk⟩

Negotek® is a registered trademark of Negotiate Ltd.

Index